SPECTRUM

Math

Grade 6

Published by Spectrum
an imprint of Carson-Dellosa Publishing LLC
Greensboro, NC

Spectrum
An imprint of Carson-Dellosa Publishing LLC
P.O. Box 35665
Greensboro, NC 27425 USA

Printed in Brimfield, OH USA • All rights reserved.   ISBN 0-7696-3696-9

8 9 10 11 12 13 HPS 13 12 11 10   12710004453

Table of Contents Grade 6

Table of Contents, continued

Check What You Know

Adding and Subtracting through 6 Digits

Add or Subtract.

	a	b	c	d	e
1.	348 +219 567	1942 +7356 9298	846 +7311	29117 +23113	211738 + 92802
2.	837 -424 413	765 -528 237	221 -119	869 -284	178 - 89
3.	873 421 +535 1829	6173 1712 +2523 10408	16082 23511 +32681	78168 3133 + 688	819293 42808 + 32122
4.	8317 -2534 5783	4468 -3275 1193	7363 -3489	3673 -2888	9472 -3715
5.	428 391 727 +126 1672	1573 2614 2418 +3903 10508	23191 12411 32408 +10803	12167 4323 1501 + 313	3250 1234 601 + 313
6.	26189 -18341 7848	45293 -28767 16526	15248 - 9312	46318 -22450	65988 -34592
7.	668924 - 84403 584521	227819 -219234 8585	466224 - 68506	588212 - 31753	100000 - 52500
8.	721 373 118 312 +126 1650	360 1300 321 +402 2383	1538 2225 1104 + 214	257 110 105 152 +440	243 -196

Check What You Know

SHOW YOUR WORK

Adding and Subtracting through 6 Digits

Solve each problem.

9. The attendance at a 3-day music festival was 297 for day 1, 363 for day 2, and 394 for day 3. What was the total attendance? What was the difference between the highest and lowest attendance?

   The total attendance was _____. The difference

   between the highest and lowest attendance was

   _____.

9.

10. When José's family started on a car trip, he noticed that the odometer reading was 23,518 miles. When they arrived home, the reading was 24,201 miles. How many miles did José's family travel?

    José's family traveled _____ miles.

10.

11. The population of Daytona Beach, Florida, is about 64,600. The population of Orlando, Florida, is about 193,700. What is the total number of people in both cities? How many more people live in Orlando?

    The total number of people in both cities is _____.

    _____ more people live in Orlando.

11.

12. January's average temperature in San Francisco, California, is 49 degrees. In Boston, Massachusetts, January's average temperature is 29 degrees. What is the difference between the two average temperatures?

    The difference between the two average temperatures

    is _____ degrees.

12.

13. Mario needs to accumulate 500 points to enter a raffle to win a bicycle. He already has 328 points. How many more points does Mario need?

    Mario needs _____ more points to enter the raffle.

13.

Lesson 1.1 Adding and Subtracting 2 and 3 Digits

```
  5 7                    2 8 3
+ 3 9                  −   4 8
-----                  -------
```

Add the ones.   Add the tens.   Rename 283 as   Subtract the ones.
Rename 16 as "1 ten   "2 hundreds,   Subtract the tens.
and 6 ones."   7 tens, and 13 ones."   Subtract the hundreds.

```
    7           1                      7 13
              5 7  addend          2 8 3  minuend
+   9       + 3 9  addend        −   4 8  subtrahend
-----       -----                -------
1 6  or 10 + 6    9 6  sum          2 3 5  difference
```

Add or subtract.

	a	b	c	d	e	f
1.	4 8 + 5 3	2 6 4 + 1 8 8	3 2 5 + 6 8	7 3 + 2 4	2 2 4 + 1 0 2	5 7 + 7 2 4
2.	7 8 − 3 3	2 5 3 − 2 0 8	2 6 2 − 2 5	5 4 0 − 2 7 8	9 3 − 3 7	2 7 − 1 9
3.	7 6 3 + 1 2 5	1 6 4 + 3 8	3 3 3 + 6 7	2 4 2 + 3 2 5	9 8 + 2 7	3 3 3 + 1 8 8
4.	8 7 4 − 2 2 2	7 2 − 5 8	8 2 − 5 6	4 8 4 − 2 9 6	4 5 4 − 3 1 9	8 4 − 4 9
5.	2 5 + 8 8	8 2 1 + 1 4 8	1 1 8 + 3 8 5	1 8 + 9 4	2 7 + 8 8	5 2 8 + 8 8
6.	8 8 − 2 5	8 2 1 − 1 4 8	1 1 8 − 8 5	5 4 0 − 2 7 8	8 8 − 2 7	5 2 8 − 3 6 2

Lesson 1.2 Adding and Subtracting 3 and 4 Digits

```
  1 1
  3 1 3 7   addend
+ 2 4 7 8   addend
─────────
  5 6 1 5   sum
```

Add the ones and rename 15 as
"1 ten and 5 ones."
Add the tens and rename 11 tens
as 1 hundred and 1 ten."
Add the hundreds.
Add the thousands.

```
    6 15 13
  4 7 6 3   minuend
─   5 8 4   subtrahend
─────────
  4 1 7 9   difference
```

Rename 63 as "5 tens and 13 ones."
Subtract the ones.
Rename 7 hundred as
"6 hundreds + 15 tens."
Subtract the tens.
Subtract the hundreds.
Subtract the thousands.

Add or subtract.

	a	b	c	d	e
1.	2175 + 362	1622 +2175	2068 +3259	368 +1436	2608 +1007
2.	2362 − 175	6586 − 244	1068 − 931	1483 −1321	2068 −1982
3.	3162 +4391	4275 +2186	1322 +1088	8166 +1253	3867 +2432
4.	1068 − 275	2222 − 252	4568 −2336	7174 −3532	2528 −2448
5.	268 +1792	513 +2170	896 +1228	358 +3178	465 +2095
6.	1293 −1025	4869 −2152	3131 −2025	8876 −3541	9412 −8637

Lesson 1.3 Adding and Subtracting 4 through 6 Digits

Add. Rename and "carry" as necessary.

```
  1 1 1 1
  2 1 3 7 5 8   addend
+   2 8 6 4 7   addend
  _____
  2 4 2 4 0 5   sum
```

Subtract. Rename each place as necessary.

```
  1 7 15 14 11
  3 X  5  4 11
  4 8 6 5 2 1   minuend
–   9 9 6 4 4   subtrahend
  _____
  3 8 6 8 7 7   difference
```

Add or subtract.

	a	b	c	d	e

1.

a	b	c	d	e
21369 + 3438	14862 +31728	15868 + 2315	25944 +31314	25144 + 8896

2.

a	b	c	d	e
27638 – 4427	48652 – 3947	29248 – 6867	84688 – 9749	26833 – 9595

3.

a	b	c	d	e
248632 + 33941	482961 + 38248	186045 + 13133	587204 + 86482	208064 + 79402

4.

a	b	c	d	e
45848 –29638	75916 –64825	64686 –28831	13812 –12436	29849 –15238

5.

a	b	c	d	e
213722 +438379	108211 +643138	112246 +232112	681249 +205863	210537 +388196

6.

a	b	c	d	e
439738 – 84325	268432 – 93341	336825 – 48930	246838 – 23704	688439 – 68257

7.

a	b	c	d	e
215862 –108291	333922 –271608	484626 –148318	689247 –213724	186398 –104793

Lesson 1.4 Adding 3 or More Numbers
(3 through 6 digits)

```
  1 1 2 2
  2 3 5 9 5
  1 6 2 3 7
  3 0 4 3 2
+ 3 1 6 3 9
-----------
1 0 1 9 0 3
```

Add the ones.	Add the tens.	Add the hundreds.	Add the thousands.	Add the ten thousands.
5	2	2	1	1
7	9	5	3	2
2	3	2	6	1
9	3	4	0	3
‒‒	3	6	1	3
23	‒‒	‒‒	‒‒	‒‒
	20	19	11	10

| Rename as "2 tens and 3 ones." | Rename as "2 hundreds and 0 tens." | Rename as "1 thousand and 9 hundreds." | Rename as "1 ten thousand and 1 thousand." | |

Add.

	a	b	c	d	e
1.	2532 17621 +20493	218932 73104 + 2068	48230 7219 +25736	298 1436 +2404	27942 31685 + 2228
2.	26731 12086 2755 +43016	5866 2311 403 +21386	3375 2839 1402 +1266	15943 10204 52113 +21308	2857 1386 215 +3108
3.	7142 302 5318 10101 + 2121	12131 43181 7624 12444 +23722	248 377 116 595 +247	7512 168 1032 745 + 2118	216842 314022 7130 21625 + 800
4.	2175 10363 1418 + 2333	15822 11317 20125 +32216	231 1486 2063 + 151	10862 11397 2133 + 4086	25382 11080 31725 +46802

Lesson 1.5 Addition and Subtraction Practice

Add or subtract.

	a	b	c	d	e
1.	237 + 846	2149 + 3765	486 + 3117	19217 + 33121	112873 + 29208
2.	738 − 244	657 − 582	212 − 104	968 − 324	188 − 79
3.	783 214 + 553	7163 1172 + 2235	10682 21315 + 32168	76188 2133 + 868	812939 42108 + 31222
4.	7138 − 2453	4648 − 3725	6733 − 3904	7633 − 2018	9742 − 3175
5.	824 319 277 + 162	1753 2164 4418 + 2903	21391 14211 30402 + 11308	16127 4233 1050 + 212	3520 1324 106 + 212
6.	21689 − 13211	54923 − 27888	18254 − 9231	48631 − 24520	56898 − 43259
7.	686492 − 48304	272189 − 217324	444662 − 86056	588212 − 31573	200000 − 25200
8.	271 733 108 213 + 117	270 1200 123 + 204	1385 2117 1208 + 124	275 106 110 215 + 550	258 − 187

Lesson 1.6 Estimating Sums and Differences

Round each number to the highest place value. Then, add from right to left.

$$
\begin{array}{r}
3876 \dashrightarrow \quad 3900 \\
+\ 321 \dashrightarrow +\ 300 \\
\hline
4200
\end{array}
$$

$$
\begin{array}{r}
31845 \dashrightarrow \quad 30000 \\
+48122 \dashrightarrow +50000 \\
\hline
80000
\end{array}
$$

Round each number to the highest place value. Then, subtract from right to left.

$$
\begin{array}{r}
4905 \dashrightarrow \quad 4900 \\
-\ 886 \dashrightarrow -\ 900 \\
\hline
4000
\end{array}
$$

$$
\begin{array}{r}
58126 \dashrightarrow \quad 60000 \\
-12395 \dashrightarrow -10000 \\
\hline
50000
\end{array}
$$

Estimate each sum or difference.

	a	b	c	d
1.	89 + 37	258 + 62	5250 +3132	23826 + 7329
2.	78 − 37	368 −142	6781 −3872	86745 −48112
3.	89 +93	819 +725	3784 +5889	93295 +18458

SHOW YOUR WORK

Estimate the answers. Then, find the exact answers.

4. Mr. Grant's class is working on a recycling project. The students are collecting aluminum cans. Over 3 days, they collected 88 cans, 113 cans, and 73 cans. About how many cans did they collect?

   The students collected about _____ cans.

   The students collected exactly _____ cans.

4.

5. There are 868 male students and 1,187 female students at Madison Middle School. About how many more female students are there than male students?

   There are about _____ more females than males.

   There are exactly _____ more females than males.

5.

Check What You Learned

Adding and Subtracting through 6 Digits

Add or subtract.

	a	b	c	d	e
1.	327 +486	5492 +3365	648 +1317	27119 +32331	238117 + 82202
2.	747 -488	567 -283	347 -229	698 -489	176 - 98
3.	387 142 +355	3716 2711 +1588	18602 32151 +24688	71688 1313 + 664	319218 24880 + 13222
4.	3871 -2435	6484 -3725	3367 -2849	7633 -2818	7294 -3517
5.	284 193 772 +128	1375 1426 1842 +1902	30951 11422 21804 +10083	17122 3432 1224 + 408	2530 1423 522 + 115
6.	29618 -21439	43295 -28387	12458 - 6813	43813 -25402	64125 -43268
7.	642896 - 87859	288172 -226388	428108 - 48045	545886 - 34225	300000 - 67800

Check What You Learned

SHOW YOUR WORK

Adding and Subtracting through 6 Digits

Solve each problem.

8. The odometer on Mrs. Rodriguez' car reads 32,425 miles. She plans to drive 396 miles. Estimate the reading on her odometer when she returns.

   The odometer will read about _____ miles.

   The exact reading on Mrs. Rodriguez' odometer will

   be _____ miles.

Use this table to answer the following questions.

Student	Weight (pounds)
John	93
Monique	74
Lydia	66
Julian	82

9. Estimate the total weight of the 4 students.

   The total weight of the 4 students is about

   _____ pounds.

10. Find the exact total weight of the 4 students.

    The exact total weight of the 4 students is

    _____ pounds.

11. Estimate the difference between John's and Lydia's weights.

    The difference between John's and Lydia's weights is

    about _____ pounds.

12. Find the exact difference between John's and Lydia's weights.

    The exact difference between John's and Lydia's

    weights is _____ pounds.

8.

9.   10.

11.   12.

Check What You Know

Multiplying and Dividing Whole Numbers

Multiply or divide.

	a	b	c	d	e
1.	88 × 6	65 × 7	383 × 4	975 × 5	8126 × 3
2.	6)79	8)453	3)654	7)2382	5)3125
3.	63 × 52	79 × 81	324 × 24	892 × 36	3825 × 63
4.	28)89	14)76	33)538	42)966	25)625
5.	312 × 263	428 × 321	286 × 448	2185 × 216	3372 × 351
6.	73)6278	54)8239	48)1872	27)54702	83)96542

Check What You Know

SHOW YOUR WORK

Multiplying and Dividing Whole Numbers

Solve each problem.

7. There are 7 sixth-grade homerooms at East Side Middle School. Each homeroom has 48 students. How many sixth-grade students are at East Side Middle School?

There are _____ sixth-grade students.

7.

8. If there are 3,600 seconds in 1 hour, how many seconds are in 58 hours?

There are _____ seconds in 58 hours.

8.

9. There are 468 trading cards which will be divided equally among 9 students. How many cards will each student get?

Each student will get _____ cards.

9.

10. There are 4,512 marbles which will be divided equally among 48 students. How many marbles will each student get?

Each student will get _____ marbles.

10.

11. Janene's family will travel from Vancouver, British Columbia, to Miami, Florida. The distance between those cities is 3,505 miles. They plan to drive 300 miles each day. About how many days will they be traveling? If Janene's family drives only 200 miles each day, about how many days will they be traveling?

They will be traveling for about _____ days at 300 miles each day.

They will be traveling for about _____ days at 200 miles each day.

11.

Lesson 2.1 Multiplying 2, 3, and 4 Digits by 1 Digit

	Multiply 8 ones by 4.	Multiply 2 tens by 4 and add 3 tens.	Multiply 7 hundreds by 4 and add 1 hundred.	Multiply 3 thousand by 4 and add two thousands.

```
  2 1 3
  3 7 2 8          8           2 0           7 0 0          3 0 0 0
×       4        × 4         ×   4         ×     4        ×       4
─────────        ───         ─────         ───────        ─────────
1 4 9 1 2        3 2           8 0          2 8 0 0        1 2 0 0 0
                            +   3 0        +   1 0 0      +   2 0 0 0
                            ─────          ───────        ─────────
                            1 1 0          2 9 0 0        1 4 0 0 0
```

	3 tens and 2 ones	1 hundred and 1 ten	2 thousands and 9 hundreds	4 thousands and 1 ten thousand

---

Multiply.

	a	b	c	d	e	f
1.	73 × 3	56 × 8	77 × 5	96 × 4	25 × 9	97 × 6
2.	273 × 6	312 × 5	278 × 7	428 × 4	122 × 5	367 × 7
3.	763 × 8	693 × 6	578 × 4	989 × 3	853 × 3	478 × 9
4.	1215 × 4	2138 × 6	3155 × 2	4068 × 5	2100 × 3	1867 × 7
5.	6125 × 2	7312 × 3	8484 × 5	3167 × 2	9319 × 3	1856 × 3
6.	98 × 9	2105 × 8	733 × 4	3509 × 2	648 × 5	99 × 9

Lesson 2.2 Multiplying 2, 3, and 4 Digits by 2 Digits

	Multiply 3263 by 3.	Multiply 3263 by 40.	Add.
3263 × 43	3263 × 3 —— 9789	3263 × 40 —— 130520	3263 × 43 —— 9789 +130520 } Add. —— 140309

Multiply.

	a	b	c	d
1.	28 ×24	35 ×18	26 ×33	85 ×45
2.	482 × 26	49 ×54	263 × 84	132 × 68
3.	324 × 27	816 × 16	255 × 44	2165 × 23
4.	5150 × 22	7182 × 12	6324 × 36	4522 × 63

Lesson 2.3 Multiplying 3 and 4 Digits by 3 Digits

Multiply 3258 by 3.	Multiply 3258 by 40.	Multiply 3258 by 200.

Multiply 3258 by 3.

```
    3 2 5 8
  ×   2 4 3
    9 7 7 4
```

Multiply 3258 by 40.

```
    3 2 5 8
  ×   2 4 3
    9 7 7 4
  1 3 0 3 2 0
```

Multiply 3258 by 200.

```
      3 2 5 8
    ×   2 4 3
      9 7 7 4
  1 3 0 3 2 0  } Add.
+ 6 5 1 6 0 0
  7 9 1 6 9 4
```

Multiply.

	a	b	c	d
1.	323 ×282	189 ×212	443 ×362	295 ×276
2.	886 ×374	763 ×618	654 ×523	985 ×447
3.	2186 × 342	1898 × 475	3688 × 259	2864 × 723
4.	5182 × 276	4825 × 125	5256 × 185	3136 × 854

Lesson 2.4 Dividing 2, 3, and 4 Digits by 1 Digit

3313 is between
2800 (7 × 400) and
3500 (7 × 500), so
the hundreds digit is 4.

```
      4
 7)3 3 1 3
  -2 8 0 0
   ─────────
      5 1 3
```

513 is between
490 (7 × 70) and
560 (7 × 80), so the
tens digit is 7.

```
     4 7
 7)3 3 1 3
  -2 8 0 0
   ─────────
     5 1 3
    - 4 9 0
     ─────────
       2 3
```

23 is between 21 (7 × 3)
and 28 (7 × 4), so the ones
digit is 3. The remainder is 2.

```
     4 7 3r2  ◄─ ┐
 7)3 3 1 3      │
  -2 8 0 0      │
   ─────────    │
     5 1 3      │
    - 4 9 0     │
     ─────────  │
       2 3      │
      - 2 1     │
      ───────── │
         2 ─ ─ ─┘
```

Divide.

	a	b	c	d	e
1.	5)4 8	7)8 6	6)2 5	8)4 7	4)6 7
2.	7)3 2 3	5)2 7 1	4)6 5 4	3)2 8 8	8)3 6 1
3.	5)2 5 2 3	6)5 7 3 0	3)6 4 8 2	4)4 5 6 2	9)7 8 6 3

Lesson 2.5 Dividing 2 and 3 Digits by 2 Digits

983 is between 840 (28 × 30) and 1120 (28 × 40), so the tens digit is 3.

143 is between 140 (28 × 5) and 168 (28 × 6), so the ones digit is 5.

$$
\begin{array}{r}
3 \\
28\overline{)983} \\
-840 \quad \text{subtract} \\
\hline
143
\end{array}
$$

$$
\begin{array}{r}
3\,5r3 \\
28\overline{)983} \\
-840 \quad \text{subtract} \\
\hline
143 \\
-140 \quad \text{subtract} \\
\hline
3 \quad \text{remainder}
\end{array}
$$

Divide.

	a	b	c	d	e
1.	18)94	27)68	22)88	19)78	25)64
2.	43)88	12)84	32)865	24)768	31)913
3.	27)815	54)725	45)880	23)615	18)324

Lesson 2.6 Dividing 4 and 5 Digits by 2 Digits

37262 is between
32800 (82 × 400) and
41000 (82 × 500), so the
hundreds digit is 4.

```
        4
82)37262
 - 32800    subtract
   4462
```

4462 is between
4100 (82 × 50) and
4920 (82 × 60), so the
tens digit is 5.

```
       45
82)37262
 - 32800
    4462
  - 4100    subtract
     362
```

362 is between
328 (82 × 4) and
410 (82 × 5), so the
ones digit is 4.

```
      454r34
82)37262
 - 32800
    4462
  - 4100
     362
   - 328    subtract
      34    remainder
```

Divide.

	a	b	c	d	e
1.	56)6185	32)9984	27)3126	13)2329	22)2420
2.	45)6950	88)9944	21)5672	78)40794	65)14625
3.	36)52813	63)45675	42)34816	23)20378	18)10242

Lesson 2.7 Estimating Products and Quotients

To estimate products, round each number to its highest place value and multiply.

$$
\begin{array}{r}
5\,6\,7\,2 \\
\times\quad 2\,8\,8 \\
\end{array}
\longrightarrow
\begin{array}{r}
6\,0\,0\,0 \\
\times\quad\ \ 3\,0\,0 \\
\hline
1\,8\,0\,0\,0\,0\,0 \\
\end{array}
$$

To estimate a quotient, round the dividend to a number that is easy to divide mentally.

$$
8\overline{)6\,2\,8\,7} \longrightarrow \begin{array}{r} 8\,0\,0 \\ 8\overline{)6\,4\,0\,0} \end{array}
$$

Estimate each product or quotient.

	a	b	c	d
1.	52 × 62	48 × 23	69 × 38	29 × 41
2.	685 × 21	231 × 42	768 × 48	865 × 72
3.	722 × 386	485 × 276	318 × 288	189 × 233
4.	3372 × 48	3892 × 73	5896 × 322	2131 × 868
5.	5)386	6)495	8)305	3)145
6.	7)6126	5)3428	9)4263	8)5720

NAME _____

Lesson 2.7 Problem Solving

SHOW YOUR WORK

Estimate the answers to the following problems.

1. There are 527 sixth-grade students who will take a field trip. There are 9 buses. About how many students will be riding in each bus?

Round 527 to _____.

About _____ students will ride each bus.

2. At West Side Middle School, there are 42 classrooms with 28 desks in each. About how many desks are there?

Round 42 to _____ and round 28 to _____.

There are about _____ desks.

3. There are 563 books to be shelved in the library. Each shelf holds 7 books. About how many shelves will be used?

Round 563 to _____.

About _____ shelves will be used.

4. Mrs. Juergen's class is building a model city from craft sticks. Each house requires 267 sticks. The class will build 93 houses. About how many sticks will be needed?

Round 267 to _____ and round 93 to _____.

About _____ sticks will be needed.

5. Thirty-eight students are going on a field trip. Parents will drive. Each car can hold 4 students along with the driver. How many cars will be needed?

Round 38 to _____.

About _____ cars will be needed.

6. Jorge's family is taking a car trip to see his grandmother. The family plans to spend 3 days on the road. The distance is 687 miles. About how far must they drive each day?

Round 687 to _____.

They must drive about _____ miles each day.

1.

2.

3.

4.

5.

6.

Spectrum Math
Grade 6
20

Chapter 2, Lesson 7
Multiplying and Dividing Whole Numbers

Check What You Learned

Multiplying and Dividing Whole Numbers

Multiply or divide.

	a	**b**	**c**	**d**	**e**
1.	66 × 8	56 × 9	838 × 3	795 × 6	8621 × 4
2.	7)69	8)435	4)912	6)2836	3)1296
3.	65 ×32	71 ×89	342 × 23	829 × 64	3528 × 45
4.	29)88	16)74	38)533	34)968	35)1225
5.	213 ×362	248 ×231	628 ×484	2851 × 261	3732 × 531
6.	76)6308	45)8329	38)1862	26)45702	86)99588

Check What You Learned

Multiplying and Dividing Whole Numbers

Solve each problem.

7. There are 467 sixth-grade students at East Side Middle School. Each one needs 8 book covers. How many book covers are needed?

_____ book covers are needed.

7.

8. A book has 353 pages. How many pages are in 54 copies of the book?

There are _____ pages in 54 copies.

8.

9. There are 712 paper clips which will be divided equally and put into 8 boxes. How many clips will be put into each box?

Each box will contain _____ clips.

9.

10. There are 5,304 tacks which will be divided equally and put into 52 boxes. How many tacks will be put into each box?

Each box will contain _____ tacks.

10.

11. Jaime's family plans to drive from Boston, Massachusetts, to Los Angeles, California. The distance between those cities is 3,017 miles. The family plans to drive 300 miles each day. About how many days will they travel? If Jaime's family drives only 200 miles each day, about how many days will the travel?

They will travel for _____ days at 300 miles each day.

They will travel for _____ days at 200 miles each day.

11.

Check What You Know

Understanding Fractions

Identify each number as prime (p) or composite (c).

a   b   c   d   e

1.   5 __p__   8 __c__   2 __p__   15 __c__   19 __p__

Find the greatest common factor of the two numbers.

2.   8 and 12   5 and 3   24 and 36   14 and 63   15 and 75

__24__   __1~~5~~__   __6__   __7__   _____

8×1 $12 \cdot 1$ $5 \textcircled{1}$ $3 \textcircled{1}$ $\begin{matrix}24.1\\12.2\end{matrix}$ $6 \cdot \textcircled{6}$ 14.1 $9 \textcircled{7}$ 75.1 3.5

$\textcircled{4} 2$ 6.2 8.2 36.1 $\textcircled{7}.2$ 1.63 25.3 15.9

     $\textcircled{4}3$ $4.\textcircled{6}$ 4.9

Change each fraction to its simplest form.

3. $\frac{15}{25}$ $\dfrac{3}{5}$ $\frac{24}{36}$ $\dfrac{6}{9} = \dfrac{2}{3}$ $\frac{25}{40}$ $\dfrac{5}{8}$ $\frac{9}{12}$ $\dfrac{3}{4}$ $\frac{14}{16}$ $\dfrac{7}{8}$

Rename each pair of fractions with common denominators.

4. $\frac{3}{8}$ and $\frac{5}{12}$ $\frac{2}{3}$ and $\frac{3}{4}$ $\frac{1}{4}$ and $\frac{5}{6}$ $\frac{4}{5}$ and $\frac{1}{2}$ $\frac{2}{3}$ and $\frac{5}{7}$

$\dfrac{4}{40}$ $\dfrac{8}{9}$ $\dfrac{6}{20}$ $\dfrac{8}{5}$ $\dfrac{14}{5}$

$\dfrac{3}{8} = \dfrac{9}{24}$ $\dfrac{2}{3} = \dfrac{8}{12}$ $\dfrac{1}{4} = \dfrac{3}{12}$ $\dfrac{4}{5} = \dfrac{4}{5}$

$\dfrac{5}{12} = \dfrac{10}{24}$ $\dfrac{3}{4} = \dfrac{9}{12}$ $\dfrac{5}{6} = \dfrac{10}{12}$ $\dfrac{8}{5} = \dfrac{8}{5}$

NAME _____

Check What You Know

Understanding Fractions

Change each improper fraction to a mixed numeral.

	a	b	c	d	e
5.	$\frac{27}{5}$ $5\frac{2}{5}$	$\frac{35}{8}$ $4\frac{3}{8}$	$\frac{15}{7}$ $2\frac{1}{7}$	$\frac{25}{4}$ $6\frac{1}{4}$	$\frac{17}{3}$ $5\frac{2}{3}$

Change each mixed numeral to an improper fraction.

6. $3\frac{5}{16}$ $\frac{33}{16}$ $3\frac{3}{5}$ $\frac{18}{5}$ $3\frac{3}{7}$ $\frac{24}{7}$ $3\frac{3}{16}$ $\frac{31}{16}$ $3\frac{1}{3}$ $\frac{10}{3}$

$$\begin{array}{r} 16 \\ \times 3 \\ \hline 28 \end{array}$$

Change each mixed numeral to its simplest form.

7. $3\frac{11}{3}$ _____ $5\frac{8}{10}$ $5\frac{4}{5}$ $1\frac{7}{5}$ $2\frac{2}{5}$ $3\frac{15}{18}$ _____ $4\frac{5}{4}$ $5\frac{1}{4}$

$3 + 3\frac{2}{3}$

$6\frac{2}{3}$

$1\frac{2}{5}$

$3\frac{5}{6}$ 4 $1\frac{1}{4}$

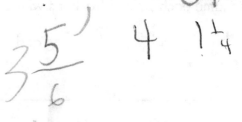

$3 + \frac{3}{18}$

3

Lesson 3.1 Prime and Composite Numbers

A **prime number** is any number greater than 1 that has only two factors, itself and 1. (Ex: 2, 3, 5, 7)

A **composite number** has more than two factors. (Ex: 4 has 3 factors, 1, 2, and 4.)

A composite number can be written as a product of prime numbers. This is called the **prime factorization** of the number. A **factor tree** is used to determine the prime factorization of the number.

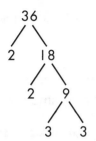

Choose any two factors to begin. Stop when all factors are prime numbers.

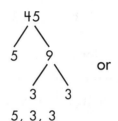

5, 3, 3   3, 3, 5

2, 2, 3, 3 is the prime factorization.

List the factors from smallest to largest.

Identify each number as prime (p) or composite (c).

	a	b	c
1.	6 _____	7 _____	13 _____
2.	19 _____	15 _____	8 _____

Use a factor tree to find the prime factorization of each number.

	a	b
3.	18	40
	_____	_____
4.	48	90
	_____	_____

Lesson 3.2 Finding the Greatest Common Factor

A factor is a divisor of a number. (For example, 3 and 4 are both factors of 12.) A **common factor** is a divisor that is shared by two or more numbers (1, 2, 4, and 8). The **greatest common factor** is the largest common factor shared by the numbers (8).

To find the greatest common factor of 32 and 40, list all of the factors of each.

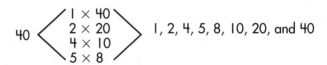

$$32 \begin{cases} 1 \times 32 \\ 2 \times 16 \\ 4 \times 8 \end{cases} 1, 2, 4, 8, 16, \text{ and } 32 \qquad 40 \begin{cases} 1 \times 40 \\ 2 \times 20 \\ 4 \times 10 \\ 5 \times 8 \end{cases} 1, 2, 4, 5, 8, 10, 20, \text{ and } 40$$

The greatest common factor is 8.

List the factors of each number below. Then, list the common factors and the greatest common factor.

		Factors	Common Factors	Greatest Common Factor
1.	8	_____	_____	_____
	12	_____		
2.	6	_____	_____	_____
	18	_____		
3.	24	_____	_____	_____
	15	_____		
4.	4	_____	_____	_____
	6	_____		
5.	5	_____	_____	_____
	12	_____		
6.	16	_____	_____	_____
	12	_____		
7.	15	_____	_____	_____
	18	_____		
8.	7	_____	_____	_____
	3	_____		

Lesson 3.3 Reducing Fractions to Their Simplest Form

A fraction is in **simplest form** when the numerator and denominator have no common factor except 1.

$\frac{16}{24} = \frac{16 \div 8}{24 \div 8} = \frac{2}{3}$

The simplest form for $\frac{16}{24}$ is $\frac{2}{3}$.

A mixed numeral is in simplest form when its fraction is in simplest form and names a number less than 1.

$2\frac{8}{10} = 2 + \frac{8 \div 2}{10 \div 2}$

$= 2 + \frac{4}{5}$

$= 2\frac{4}{5}$

The simplest form of $2\frac{8}{10}$ is $2\frac{4}{5}$.

Change each of the following to simplest form.

	a	b	c
1.	$\frac{8}{12}$ _____	$\frac{9}{24}$ _____	$\frac{10}{16}$ _____
2.	$3\frac{4}{6}$ _____	$5\frac{8}{16}$ _____	$4\frac{12}{16}$ _____
3.	$\frac{14}{16}$ _____	$\frac{10}{12}$ _____	$\frac{16}{40}$ _____
4.	$\frac{8}{30}$ _____	$\frac{21}{36}$ _____	$\frac{15}{18}$ _____
5.	$2\frac{3}{15}$ _____	$1\frac{10}{12}$ _____	$2\frac{18}{24}$ _____
6.	$\frac{12}{20}$ _____	$\frac{12}{21}$ _____	$\frac{16}{32}$ _____

Lesson 3.4 Finding Common Denominators

The two fractions $\frac{1}{5}$ and $\frac{3}{5}$ have common denominators. However $\frac{1}{4}$ and $\frac{3}{5}$ do not have common denominators. Rename these fractions so that they have common denominators by finding the least common multiple of their denominators. The **least common multiple** of two numbers is the smallest number that is a multiple of both.

Multiples of 4 are 4, 8, 12, 16, 20, 24, . . .

Multiples of 5 are 5, 10, 15, 20, . . .

The smallest number that is a multiple of 4 and 5 is 20.

Rename each fraction with a denominator of 20.

$\frac{1}{4} = \frac{1 \times 5}{4 \times 5} = \frac{5}{20}$; $\frac{3}{5} = \frac{3 \times 4}{5 \times 4} = \frac{12}{20}$

$\frac{5}{20}$ and $\frac{12}{20}$ have common denominators.

Rename each pair of fractions with common denominators.

	a	b	c
1.	$\frac{1}{4}$ and $\frac{2}{3}$ _____	$\frac{3}{8}$ and $\frac{7}{10}$ _____	$\frac{4}{7}$ and $\frac{2}{3}$ _____
2.	$\frac{3}{8}$ and $\frac{1}{6}$ _____	$\frac{2}{3}$ and $\frac{1}{2}$ _____	$\frac{3}{8}$ and $\frac{5}{6}$ _____
3.	$\frac{2}{5}$ and $\frac{1}{3}$ _____	$\frac{5}{16}$ and $\frac{3}{8}$ _____	$\frac{1}{2}$ and $\frac{1}{3}$ _____
4.	$\frac{5}{8}$ and $\frac{3}{16}$ _____	$\frac{2}{5}$ and $\frac{3}{4}$ _____	$\frac{5}{12}$ and $\frac{4}{5}$ _____
5.	$\frac{4}{9}$ and $\frac{1}{2}$ _____	$\frac{7}{8}$ and $\frac{7}{12}$ _____	$\frac{1}{9}$ and $\frac{2}{3}$ _____

Lesson 3.5 Changing Improper Fractions to Mixed Numerals

An **improper fraction** has a numerator that is larger than its denominator. $\frac{19}{8}$ is an improper fraction.

$\frac{19}{8}$ means $19 \div 8$ or

$$8)\overline{19} \;\; \begin{array}{r} 2 \\ \end{array}$$
$$\begin{array}{r} -16 \\ \hline 3 \end{array} \rightarrow 3 \div 8 = \frac{3}{8}$$

This mixed numeral is written $2\frac{3}{8}$

$\frac{19}{8} = 2\frac{3}{8}$

Change each improper fraction to a mixed numeral.

	a	b	c	d
1.	$\frac{23}{5}$ _____	$\frac{13}{4}$ _____	$\frac{15}{7}$ _____	$\frac{16}{9}$ _____
2.	$\frac{25}{6}$ _____	$\frac{5}{3}$ _____	$\frac{12}{5}$ _____	$\frac{15}{4}$ _____
3.	$\frac{17}{10}$ _____	$\frac{38}{7}$ _____	$\frac{14}{5}$ _____	$\frac{8}{3}$ _____
4.	$\frac{20}{3}$ _____	$\frac{7}{6}$ _____	$\frac{5}{2}$ _____	$\frac{4}{3}$ _____
5.	$\frac{3}{2}$ _____	$\frac{7}{5}$ _____	$\frac{15}{8}$ _____	$\frac{25}{8}$ _____
6.	$\frac{11}{4}$ _____	$\frac{36}{7}$ _____	$\frac{7}{4}$ _____	$\frac{8}{5}$ _____

Lesson 3.6 Changing Mixed Numerals to Improper Fractions

To change a mixed numeral to a fraction, multiply the denominator by the whole number. Then, add the numerator to get the new numerator. Keep the denominator the same.

$$4\frac{3}{5} = \frac{(5 \times 4) + 3}{5} = \frac{20 + 3}{5} = \frac{23}{5}$$

$$2\frac{3}{4} = \frac{(4 \times 2) + 3}{4} = \frac{8 + 3}{4} = \frac{11}{4}$$

Change each mixed numeral to an improper fraction.

	a	b	c	d
1.	$2\frac{5}{8}$ _____	$3\frac{1}{4}$ _____	$2\frac{3}{7}$ _____	$4\frac{1}{2}$ _____
2.	$3\frac{3}{4}$ _____	$2\frac{5}{12}$ _____	$4\frac{1}{6}$ _____	$5\frac{2}{3}$ _____
3.	$2\frac{7}{16}$ _____	$3\frac{1}{2}$ _____	$1\frac{7}{16}$ _____	$2\frac{5}{8}$ _____
4.	$3\frac{1}{3}$ _____	$4\frac{2}{5}$ _____	$3\frac{1}{8}$ _____	$7\frac{1}{3}$ _____
5.	$8\frac{2}{3}$ _____	$1\frac{2}{5}$ _____	$2\frac{3}{7}$ _____	$3\frac{8}{9}$ _____
6.	$4\frac{2}{5}$ _____	$3\frac{5}{6}$ _____	$2\frac{4}{9}$ _____	$4\frac{5}{12}$ _____

Lesson 3.7 Simplifying Mixed Numerals

A mixed numeral is in simplest form if its fraction is in simplest form and names a number less than 1.
The greatest common factor of 8 and 12 is 4.

$$3\frac{8}{12}$$

$$3 + \frac{8 \div 4}{12 \div 4} = \frac{2}{3}$$

$$3\frac{8}{12} = 3\frac{2}{3}$$

$$2\frac{9}{4} = 2 + \frac{9}{4}$$

$$2 + (2\frac{1}{4}) = 4\frac{1}{4}$$

not in simplest form

Change each mixed numeral to simplest form.

	a	b	c	d
1.	$3\frac{6}{8}$ _____	$2\frac{12}{15}$ _____	$1\frac{9}{12}$ _____	$4\frac{10}{15}$ _____
2.	$2\frac{8}{5}$ _____	$3\frac{15}{4}$ _____	$1\frac{7}{3}$ _____	$2\frac{5}{2}$ _____
3.	$4\frac{4}{8}$ _____	$5\frac{6}{9}$ _____	$8\frac{12}{20}$ _____	$7\frac{4}{16}$ _____
4.	$2\frac{10}{4}$ _____	$3\frac{3}{2}$ _____	$7\frac{8}{12}$ _____	$5\frac{3}{9}$ _____
5.	$2\frac{10}{3}$ _____	$4\frac{6}{5}$ _____	$3\frac{15}{7}$ _____	$2\frac{20}{9}$ _____

Lesson 3.8 Problem Solving

SHOW YOUR WORK

Solve each problem.

1. Show a factor tree and determine the prime factorization of 90.

   _____

2. Find the greatest common factor of 28 and 32.

   Factors of 28 are _____.

   Factors of 32 are _____.

   The greatest common factor is_____.

3. Find the least common multiple of 8 and 6.

   Multiples of 8 are _____.

   Multiples of 6 are _____.

   The least common multiple is _____.

4. In a recent year, it rained 8 out of the 28 days in February. Write a fraction (in simplest form) showing the days in February that it rained.

   It rained _____ days.

5. Of 128 members of the school chorus, 96 are sopranos. What fraction (in simplest form) of the members of the school chorus are sopranos.

   _____ of the members of the school chorus are sopranos.

6. Darius wrote the mixed numeral $5\frac{12}{9}$ on the blackboard. What is the simplest form of that mixed numeral?

   The simplest form of that mixed numeral is _____.

1.

2.

3.

4.

5.

6.

Check What You Learned

Understanding Fractions

Identify each number as prime (p) or composite (c).

	a	b	c	d	e
I.	7 _____	21 _____	3 _____	27 _____	6 _____

Find the greatest common factor of the two numbers.

2.	16 and 24	21 and 14	9 and 45	13 and 25	12 and 45
	_____	_____	_____	_____	_____

Change each fraction to its simplest form.

3. $\frac{10}{25}$ _____ $\frac{21}{35}$ _____ $\frac{15}{24}$ _____ $\frac{16}{20}$ _____ $\frac{21}{24}$ _____

Rename each pair of fractions with common denominators.

4. $\frac{5}{8}$ and $\frac{7}{12}$ $\frac{3}{4}$ and $\frac{1}{6}$ $\frac{3}{5}$ and $\frac{2}{3}$ $\frac{3}{8}$ and $\frac{2}{3}$ $\frac{2}{7}$ and $\frac{5}{8}$

_____   _____   _____   _____   _____

Check What You Learned

Understanding Fractions

Change each improper fraction to a mixed numeral.

	a	b	c	d	e
5.	$\frac{27}{8}$ _____	$\frac{18}{5}$ _____	$\frac{19}{6}$ _____	$\frac{35}{4}$ _____	$\frac{27}{5}$ _____

Change each mixed numeral to an improper fraction.

6.	$4\frac{3}{7}$ _____	$2\frac{7}{16}$ _____	$3\frac{4}{5}$ _____	$7\frac{5}{6}$ _____	$6\frac{2}{3}$ _____

Change each mixed numeral to its simplest form.

7.	$3\frac{7}{5}$ _____	$5\frac{12}{7}$ _____	$2\frac{8}{12}$ _____	$1\frac{11}{4}$ _____	$5\frac{5}{20}$ _____

Check What You Know

Adding and Subtracting Fractions

Add or subtract. Write answers in simplest form.

	a	**b**	**c**	**d**
1.	$\frac{3}{8}$ $+\frac{7}{8}$	$\frac{4}{5}$ $+\frac{3}{5}$	$\frac{2}{3}$ $+\frac{5}{8}$	$\frac{1}{3}$ $+\frac{1}{2}$
2.	$\frac{7}{8}$ $-\frac{5}{8}$	$\frac{11}{16}$ $-\frac{5}{16}$	$\frac{3}{4}$ $-\frac{1}{3}$	$\frac{5}{6}$ $-\frac{1}{2}$
3.	$2\frac{5}{8}$ $+1\frac{2}{3}$	$3\frac{1}{3}$ $+2\frac{3}{4}$	$5\frac{2}{5}$ $+2\frac{2}{3}$	$7\frac{2}{7}$ $+3\frac{1}{2}$
4.	$7\frac{2}{3}$ $-3\frac{1}{8}$	$6\frac{5}{6}$ $-2\frac{3}{4}$	$5\frac{1}{2}$ $-3\frac{2}{3}$	4 $-1\frac{3}{5}$
5.	$1\frac{3}{8}$ $2\frac{1}{3}$ $+\frac{5}{6}$	$2\frac{1}{8}$ $1\frac{1}{2}$ $+3\frac{1}{4}$	$3\frac{1}{2}$ $4\frac{1}{3}$ $+1\frac{3}{4}$	$2\frac{2}{5}$ $1\frac{1}{3}$ $+\frac{4}{5}$

NAME _____

Check What You Know

SHOW YOUR WORK

Adding and Subtracting Fractions

Solve each problem. Write answers in simplest form.

6. Rosa needs to mail two packages. One weighs $\frac{5}{8}$ of a pound and the other weighs $\frac{2}{3}$ of a pound. What is the total weight of the two packages? How much heavier is Rosa's second package than the first?

The total weight of the two packages is _____.

The second package weighs _____ pound more.

6.

7. Dylan played tennis for $1\frac{1}{3}$ hours on Sunday. On Tuesday, he played for $2\frac{1}{2}$ hours. How many total hours did he play on those two days? How much longer did Dylan play on Tuesday than on Sunday?

Dylan played for a total of _____ hours.

He played for _____ more hours on Tuesday.

7.

8. Daniel spent $1\frac{2}{3}$ hours raking leaves on Monday. On Tuesday, he raked for $1\frac{1}{2}$ hours. How many total hours did Daniel rake on those two days?

Daniel raked for _____ total hours.

8.

9. A radio battery will last for $5\frac{1}{3}$ hours. The radio has been played for $3\frac{3}{4}$ hours. How much longer should the battery last?

The battery should last _____ hours more.

9.

Lesson 4.1 Adding Fractions with Like Denominators

$$\begin{array}{r} \frac{7}{8} \\ + \ \frac{3}{8} \\ \hline \frac{10}{8} = \frac{5}{4} = 1\frac{1}{4} \end{array}$$

Add the numerators.

Use the same denominator.

Change to simplest form.

Add. Write answers in simplest form.

	a	b	c	d	e
1.	$\frac{3}{5}$ $+ \ \frac{4}{5}$	$\frac{1}{4}$ $+ \ \frac{3}{4}$	$\frac{2}{3}$ $+ \ \frac{2}{3}$	$\frac{5}{6}$ $+ \ \frac{3}{6}$	$\frac{3}{10}$ $+ \ \frac{9}{10}$
2.	$\frac{5}{7}$ $+ \ \frac{3}{7}$	$\frac{4}{9}$ $+ \ \frac{2}{9}$	$\frac{3}{4}$ $+ \ \frac{3}{4}$	$\frac{5}{6}$ $+ \ \frac{4}{6}$	$\frac{3}{10}$ $+ \ \frac{5}{10}$
3.	$\frac{1}{3}$ $+ \ \frac{1}{3}$	$\frac{5}{8}$ $+ \ \frac{7}{8}$	$\frac{5}{6}$ $+ \ \frac{2}{6}$	$\frac{8}{9}$ $+ \ \frac{5}{9}$	$\frac{5}{7}$ $+ \ \frac{4}{7}$
4.	$\frac{2}{5}$ $+ \ \frac{4}{5}$	$\frac{3}{4}$ $+ \ \frac{1}{4}$	$\frac{2}{7}$ $+ \ \frac{6}{7}$	$\frac{2}{5}$ $+ \ \frac{1}{5}$	$\frac{3}{8}$ $+ \ \frac{6}{8}$
5.	$\frac{3}{4}$ $+ \ \frac{2}{4}$	$\frac{3}{5}$ $+ \ \frac{4}{5}$	$\frac{7}{10}$ $+ \ \frac{9}{10}$	$\frac{3}{7}$ $+ \ \frac{6}{7}$	$\frac{7}{8}$ $+ \ \frac{7}{8}$

Lesson 4.2 Subtracting Fractions with Like Denominators

$$\begin{array}{r} \frac{5}{8} \\ -\ \frac{3}{8} \\ \hline \frac{2}{8} = \frac{1}{4} \end{array}$$ Subtract the numerators.
Use the same denominator.
Change to simplest form.

Subtract. Write answers in simplest form.

	a	**b**	**c**	**d**	**e**
1.	$\frac{5}{6}$ $-\frac{1}{6}$	$\frac{7}{8}$ $-\frac{1}{8}$	$\frac{3}{4}$ $-\frac{1}{4}$	$\frac{5}{9}$ $-\frac{1}{9}$	$\frac{7}{8}$ $-\frac{3}{8}$
2.	$\frac{2}{3}$ $-\frac{1}{3}$	$\frac{4}{6}$ $-\frac{1}{6}$	$\frac{8}{9}$ $-\frac{5}{9}$	$\frac{7}{8}$ $-\frac{5}{8}$	$\frac{5}{7}$ $-\frac{3}{7}$
3.	$\frac{9}{10}$ $-\frac{7}{10}$	$\frac{4}{5}$ $-\frac{2}{5}$	$\frac{5}{6}$ $-\frac{2}{6}$	$\frac{7}{8}$ $-\frac{4}{8}$	$\frac{4}{9}$ $-\frac{1}{9}$
4.	$\frac{7}{12}$ $-\frac{5}{12}$	$\frac{11}{12}$ $-\frac{5}{12}$	$\frac{7}{12}$ $-\frac{1}{12}$	$\frac{8}{9}$ $-\frac{2}{9}$	$\frac{11}{12}$ $-\frac{7}{12}$
5.	$\frac{9}{10}$ $-\frac{3}{10}$	$\frac{5}{8}$ $-\frac{2}{8}$	$\frac{3}{6}$ $-\frac{1}{6}$	$\frac{11}{12}$ $-\frac{1}{12}$	$\frac{5}{7}$ $-\frac{2}{7}$

Lesson 4.3 Adding and Subtracting with Unlike Denominators

Rename fractions with the lowest common denominator. Change to simplest form.

20 = least
common multiple

$$\begin{array}{r} \frac{4}{5} \frac{(\times 4)}{(\times 4)} = \frac{16}{20} \\ + \frac{3}{4} \frac{(\times 5)}{(\times 5)} = \frac{15}{20} \\ \hline \frac{31}{20} = 1\frac{11}{20} \end{array}$$

12 = least
common multiple

$$\begin{array}{r} \frac{3}{4} \frac{(\times 3)}{(\times 3)} = \frac{9}{12} \\ - \frac{5}{12} \quad\quad = \frac{5}{12} \\ \hline \frac{4}{12} = \frac{1}{3} \end{array}$$

Add or subtract. Write answers in simplest form.

	a	b	c	d	e
1.	$\frac{5}{8} + \frac{3}{4}$	$\frac{5}{6} + \frac{3}{5}$	$\frac{2}{3} + \frac{3}{4}$	$\frac{7}{10} + \frac{1}{2}$	$\frac{3}{8} + \frac{2}{3}$
2.	$\frac{3}{4} - \frac{5}{8}$	$\frac{7}{10} - \frac{1}{2}$	$\frac{7}{8} - \frac{1}{2}$	$\frac{3}{4} - \frac{1}{3}$	$\frac{5}{9} - \frac{1}{3}$
3.	$\frac{5}{12} + \frac{5}{6}$	$\frac{3}{8} + \frac{3}{4}$	$\frac{7}{9} + \frac{2}{3}$	$\frac{5}{8} + \frac{1}{6}$	$\frac{2}{3} + \frac{7}{10}$
4.	$\frac{3}{4} - \frac{2}{3}$	$\frac{9}{10} - \frac{2}{5}$	$\frac{5}{8} - \frac{1}{4}$	$\frac{5}{6} - \frac{1}{4}$	$\frac{5}{6} - \frac{3}{4}$

Lesson 4.4 Adding Mixed Numerals with Unlike Denominators

$2\frac{1}{2}\,^{(\times\,4)}_{(\times\,4)}$ $2\frac{4}{8}$ Rename fractions with common denominators. $3\frac{3}{4}\,^{(\times\,2)}_{(\times\,2)}$ $3\frac{6}{8}$

$+3\frac{3}{8}$ $+3\frac{3}{8}$ Add the fractions. Add the whole numbers. $+2\frac{5}{8}$ $+2\frac{5}{8}$

$5\frac{7}{8}$ Simplify. $5\frac{11}{8} = 6\frac{3}{8}$

$5 + 1\frac{3}{8} = 6\frac{3}{8}$

Add. Write answers in simplest form.

	a	**b**	**c**	**d**
1.	$3\frac{2}{5}$	$7\frac{3}{8}$	$4\frac{1}{2}$	$5\frac{1}{2}$
	$+2\frac{3}{10}$	$+\ \frac{3}{4}$	$+2\frac{2}{3}$	$+\ \frac{5}{6}$
2.	$2\frac{3}{4}$	$2\frac{1}{2}$	$3\frac{2}{3}$	$1\frac{1}{8}$
	$+1\frac{1}{6}$	$+3\frac{5}{8}$	$+\ \frac{5}{6}$	$+3\frac{3}{4}$
3.	$1\frac{1}{2}$	$2\frac{3}{8}$	$\frac{2}{3}$	$2\frac{3}{8}$
	$2\frac{1}{3}$	$3\frac{1}{4}$	$1\frac{1}{2}$	$3\frac{1}{2}$
	$+\ \frac{3}{4}$	$+2\frac{1}{2}$	$+2\frac{1}{4}$	$+1\frac{1}{4}$
4.	$2\frac{1}{6}$	$\frac{5}{6}$	$3\frac{5}{8}$	$1\frac{2}{3}$
	$3\frac{2}{3}$	$2\frac{1}{3}$	$2\frac{1}{4}$	$3\frac{1}{2}$
	$+1\frac{1}{2}$	$+\ \frac{2}{3}$	$+2\frac{1}{2}$	$+1\frac{3}{5}$

Lesson 4.5 Subtracting Mixed Numerals with Unlike Denominators

$$5\frac{3}{4} \; {\scriptstyle(\times 3) \atop (\times 3)} = \quad 5\frac{9}{12}$$
$$-2\frac{2}{3} \; {\scriptstyle(\times 4) \atop (\times 4)} = -2\frac{8}{12}$$
$$\overline{\qquad\qquad\quad 3\frac{1}{12}}$$

Rename.

$$4\frac{1}{3} = 3 + 1\frac{1}{3} = 3\frac{4}{3}$$
$$-1\frac{2}{3} \qquad\qquad -1\frac{2}{3}$$
$$\overline{\qquad\qquad\qquad\quad 2\frac{2}{3}}$$

Subtract. Write answers in simplest form.

	a	**b**	**c**	**d**
1.	4 $-\frac{3}{8}$	$5\frac{5}{6}$ $-1\frac{1}{3}$	8 $-3\frac{5}{8}$	$4\frac{3}{5}$ $-\frac{3}{10}$
2.	$5\frac{3}{4}$ $-4\frac{5}{8}$	$8\frac{2}{3}$ $-4\frac{1}{6}$	$5\frac{5}{6}$ $-3\frac{3}{4}$	$7\frac{4}{5}$ $-2\frac{1}{2}$
3.	$5\frac{3}{8}$ $-2\frac{7}{8}$	$3\frac{1}{4}$ $-2\frac{3}{4}$	$8\frac{2}{5}$ $-3\frac{4}{5}$	$1\frac{1}{3}$ $-\frac{2}{3}$
4.	$4\frac{3}{4}$ $-2\frac{7}{8}$	$6\frac{1}{2}$ $-3\frac{2}{3}$	5 $-2\frac{3}{5}$	3 $-\frac{5}{6}$

Lesson 4.6 Problem Solving

SHOW YOUR WORK

Solve each problem. Write answers in simplest form.

1. Nadine spent $\frac{3}{4}$ of an hour on her math homework and $\frac{2}{3}$ of an hour on science. How much time did she study the two subjects? How much more time did Nadine spend on mathematics than on science?

   Nadine studied the two subjects for _____ hours.

   Nadine spent _____ of an hour more on mathematics.

2. Sam studied for $1\frac{3}{4}$ hours on Tuesday and $1\frac{1}{3}$ hours Wednesday. How many total hours did Sam study those on two days?

   Sam studied for _____ hours.

3. A recipe calls for $2\frac{1}{3}$ cups of flour and $1\frac{1}{4}$ cups of sugar. What is the amount of flour and sugar together?

   The amount of flour and sugar together is

   _____ cups.

4. The CD in the player will play for two hours. It has been playing for $\frac{1}{3}$ of an hour. How much longer does it have to play?

   It will play for an additional _____ hours.

5. Carlota needs to practice the piano for $1\frac{2}{3}$ hours. She has been practicing for $\frac{3}{4}$ of an hour. How much longer must she practice?

   She must practice for _____ of an hour longer.

6. Ferris started to bike the $4\frac{1}{3}$ miles to school. After $\frac{3}{5}$ mile, he stopped to talk to a friend. How much farther did he have to go to get to school?

   Ferris had to ride _____ miles.

1.

2.

3.

4.

5.

6.

Check What You Learned

Adding and Subtracting Fractions

Add or subtract. Write answers in simplest form.

	a	**b**	**c**	**d**
1.	$\frac{4}{3}$ $+\frac{4}{3}$	$\frac{3}{8}$ $+\frac{2}{3}$	$\frac{1}{3}$ $+\frac{1}{4}$	$\frac{2}{5}$ $+\frac{3}{4}$
2.	$\frac{9}{16}$ $-\frac{3}{16}$	$\frac{5}{6}$ $-\frac{5}{8}$	$\frac{3}{4}$ $-\frac{3}{5}$	$\frac{7}{8}$ $-\frac{2}{5}$
3.	$2\frac{3}{8}$ $+3\frac{1}{3}$	$1\frac{1}{4}$ $+2\frac{5}{6}$	$5\frac{3}{8}$ $+3\frac{1}{2}$	$4\frac{4}{7}$ $+3\frac{2}{3}$
4.	$6\frac{3}{4}$ $-2\frac{2}{3}$	$2\frac{5}{7}$ $-1\frac{2}{3}$	$4\frac{1}{2}$ $-1\frac{5}{6}$	7 $-3\frac{4}{7}$
5.	$3\frac{5}{8}$ $1\frac{2}{3}$ $+\ \frac{1}{6}$	$2\frac{5}{6}$ $3\frac{1}{2}$ $+2\frac{1}{3}$	$5\frac{1}{2}$ $4\frac{1}{6}$ $+2\frac{3}{4}$	$1\frac{3}{5}$ $1\frac{1}{3}$ $+2\frac{4}{5}$

Check What You Learned

Adding and Subtracting Fractions

Solve each problem. Write answers in simplest form.

6. Luis mowed $\frac{1}{3}$ of the lawn and Jorge mowed $\frac{3}{8}$ of the lawn. What was the total part of the lawn that they mowed together? Did Luis or Jorge mow a larger part of the lawn? How much more?

Together they mowed _____ of the lawn.

_____ mowed a larger part of the lawn.

He mowed _____ more.

6.

7. Maria babysat her brothers for $1\frac{2}{3}$ hours on Monday and $2\frac{1}{2}$ hours on Wednesday. How many total hours did she babysit on those two days? How much longer did she babysit on Wednesday than on Monday?

She babysat for _____ hours.

She babysat _____ of an hour more on Wednesday.

7.

8. Miki is making bows. She needs $5\frac{3}{4}$ inches for one and $3\frac{2}{3}$ inches for the other. How much ribbon does she need for both bows?

She needs _____ inches.

8.

9. Carla has a length of ribbon that is 14 inches long. How much will be left if she uses $10\frac{1}{4}$ inches of it?

_____ inches of ribbon will be left.

9.

10. On Monday, Paula bought $12\frac{1}{8}$ gallons of gas for her car. On Friday, she bought another $6\frac{3}{5}$ gallons. How many gallons did she buy on these two days?

Paula bought _____ gallons of gas.

10.

NAME _____

Check What You Know

Multiplying and Dividing Fractions

Multiply or divide. Write answers in simplest form.

	a	b	c
1.	$\frac{7}{8} \times \frac{3}{4}$	$9 \times \frac{3}{8}$	$\frac{5}{8} \times 5$
2.	$3\frac{1}{8} \times 4$	$8 \times 2\frac{3}{5}$	$4\frac{1}{2} \times 9$
3.	$5\frac{3}{4} \times 2\frac{1}{3}$	$2\frac{1}{4} \times 3\frac{1}{5}$	$3\frac{2}{3} \times 1\frac{1}{8}$
4.	$8 \div \frac{2}{3}$	$\frac{4}{5} \div 3$	$10 \div \frac{3}{8}$
5.	$\frac{4}{5} \div \frac{7}{8}$	$\frac{2}{3} \div \frac{5}{6}$	$\frac{3}{8} \div \frac{7}{8}$
6.	$2\frac{3}{4} \div 3\frac{1}{8}$	$7 \div 3\frac{1}{4}$	$7\frac{3}{8} \div 9$

Check What You Know

SHOW YOUR WORK

Multiplying and Dividing Fractions

Solve each problem. Write answers in simplest form.

7. John and George together raked $\frac{7}{8}$ of the yard. John raked $\frac{3}{4}$ of that amount. What part of the yard did John rake?

   George raked _____ of the yard.

   7.

8. Felipe has track practice for $\frac{5}{8}$ of an hour after school each day. How many hours does he have track practice in 5 days?

   Felipe has track practice for _____ hours.

   8.

9. Paul can walk $2\frac{1}{2}$ miles in 1 hour. How far can he walk in $1\frac{3}{4}$ hours?

   Paul can walk _____ miles.

   9.

10. Brad has a stack of 7 books on his desk. Each book is $1\frac{7}{8}$ inches thick. How tall is the stack?

    The stack is _____ inches tall.

    10.

11. A bag of candy weighs $3\frac{2}{3}$ ounces. How much would $4\frac{1}{2}$ bags of candy weigh?

    The bags would weigh _____ ounces.

    11.

12. It takes 8 hours to paint a room. How long will it take to paint $\frac{2}{3}$ of the room?

    It will take _____ hours to paint $\frac{2}{3}$ of the room.

    12.

13. Jim will divide $6\frac{3}{4}$ pounds of candy equally among 9 friends. How much candy will each friend get?

    Each friend will get _____ of a pound.

    13.

Lesson 5.1 Multiplying Fractions

Multiply fractions.

$\frac{3}{8} \times \frac{2}{3} = \frac{3 \times 2}{8 \times 3}$ Multiply numerators together. Multiply denominators together.

$\quad = \frac{6}{24} = \frac{1}{4}$ Simplify.

Multiply. Write answers in simplest form.

	a	b	c	d
1.	$\frac{2}{5} \times \frac{2}{3}$	$\frac{3}{4} \times \frac{5}{6}$	$\frac{7}{8} \times \frac{5}{7}$	$\frac{2}{5} \times \frac{3}{4}$
2.	$\frac{7}{12} \times \frac{3}{4}$	$\frac{2}{3} \times \frac{8}{9}$	$\frac{4}{5} \times \frac{3}{8}$	$\frac{3}{7} \times \frac{3}{5}$
3.	$\frac{1}{6} \times \frac{2}{3}$	$\frac{11}{12} \times \frac{2}{3}$	$\frac{2}{5} \times \frac{2}{5}$	$\frac{3}{4} \times \frac{3}{7}$
4.	$\frac{2}{9} \times \frac{3}{8}$	$\frac{5}{8} \times \frac{1}{6}$	$\frac{8}{9} \times \frac{2}{3}$	$\frac{7}{8} \times \frac{7}{8}$
5.	$\frac{5}{9} \times \frac{7}{8}$	$\frac{3}{4} \times \frac{3}{4}$	$\frac{3}{8} \times \frac{3}{5}$	$\frac{3}{7} \times \frac{2}{5}$
6.	$\frac{1}{3} \times \frac{3}{7}$	$\frac{1}{4} \times \frac{1}{2}$	$\frac{4}{5} \times \frac{3}{4}$	$\frac{7}{8} \times \frac{2}{9}$

Lesson 5.2 Multiplying Fractions and Whole Numbers

$\frac{3}{5} \times 8$

$\frac{3}{5} \times \frac{8}{1} = \frac{24}{5}$ Rename 8 as $\frac{8}{1}$.

    $= 4\frac{4}{5}$ Write in simplest form.

$5 \times \frac{2}{3}$

$\frac{5}{1} \times \frac{2}{3} = \frac{10}{3}$ Rename 5 as $\frac{5}{1}$.

    $= 3\frac{1}{3}$ Write in simplest form.

Multiply. Write answers in simplest form.

	a	b	c	d
1.	$3 \times \frac{5}{8}$	$8 \times \frac{4}{5}$	$6 \times \frac{2}{3}$	$4 \times \frac{7}{8}$
2.	$\frac{3}{5} \times 6$	$\frac{5}{12} \times 9$	$\frac{3}{7} \times 4$	$\frac{5}{8} \times 6$
3.	$10 \times \frac{2}{5}$	$5 \times \frac{5}{8}$	$3 \times \frac{4}{7}$	$2 \times \frac{3}{4}$
4.	$\frac{3}{10} \times 8$	$\frac{2}{3} \times 7$	$\frac{3}{4} \times 9$	$\frac{1}{2} \times 5$
5.	$9 \times \frac{1}{3}$	$2 \times \frac{7}{16}$	$\frac{2}{3} \times 2$	$\frac{3}{8} \times 5$

Lesson 5.3 Multiplying Mixed Numbers and Whole Numbers

$2\frac{3}{4} \times 5$ Rename the mixed number and the whole number as improper fractions.

$\frac{11}{4} \times \frac{5}{1}$ Multiply.

$= \frac{55}{4} = 13\frac{3}{4}$ Write in simplest form.

Multiply. Write answers in simplest form.

	a	b	c	d
1.	$1\frac{1}{2} \times 5$	$2\frac{1}{4} \times 3$	$8 \times 3\frac{1}{2}$	$4 \times 3\frac{1}{2}$
2.	$7 \times 3\frac{3}{8}$	$6 \times 2\frac{3}{4}$	$2\frac{1}{3} \times 4$	$3\frac{1}{8} \times 5$
3.	$1\frac{1}{4} \times 6$	$3\frac{1}{2} \times 7$	$5 \times 2\frac{1}{8}$	$4 \times 2\frac{1}{4}$
4.	$2 \times 2\frac{3}{7}$	$8 \times 4\frac{3}{5}$	$2\frac{1}{3} \times 3$	$5\frac{3}{8} \times 2$
5.	$1\frac{3}{4} \times 7$	$1\frac{5}{8} \times 6$	$3 \times 2\frac{1}{4}$	$4 \times 6\frac{1}{2}$

Lesson 5.4 Multiplying Mixed Numbers

$2\frac{3}{4} \times 3\frac{1}{3}$ Rename each mixed numeral as an improper fraction.

$\frac{11}{4} \times \frac{10}{3} = \frac{110}{12} = \frac{55}{6}$ Multiply.

$= 9\frac{1}{6}$ Simplify.

Multiply. Write answers in simplest form.

	a	b	c	d
1.	$1\frac{1}{3} \times 2\frac{1}{8}$	$2\frac{1}{2} \times 1\frac{3}{4}$	$2\frac{5}{8} \times 2\frac{3}{5}$	$1\frac{1}{2} \times 2\frac{2}{3}$
2.	$3\frac{1}{5} \times 5\frac{2}{3}$	$4\frac{1}{2} \times 4\frac{1}{2}$	$2\frac{1}{3} \times 3\frac{1}{4}$	$2\frac{4}{5} \times 3\frac{1}{8}$
3.	$2\frac{2}{3} \times 5\frac{1}{4}$	$2\frac{1}{3} \times 2\frac{1}{3}$	$3\frac{1}{4} \times 1\frac{1}{8}$	$2\frac{7}{8} \times 1\frac{1}{3}$
4.	$2\frac{5}{8} \times 2\frac{1}{4}$	$1\frac{1}{8} \times 1\frac{3}{5}$	$1\frac{1}{6} \times 2\frac{3}{8}$	$4\frac{1}{2} \times 3\frac{1}{3}$
5.	$1\frac{3}{5} \times 2\frac{5}{8}$	$1\frac{2}{3} \times 3\frac{2}{3}$	$2\frac{1}{2} \times 1\frac{3}{5}$	$2\frac{2}{3} \times 1\frac{5}{8}$

Lesson 5.5 Multiplication Practice

Multiply. Write answers in simplest form.

	a	b	c	d
1.	$\frac{2}{3} \times \frac{4}{5}$	$\frac{3}{8} \times \frac{5}{8}$	$\frac{2}{7} \times \frac{4}{5}$	$\frac{2}{3} \times \frac{3}{8}$
2.	$\frac{1}{2} \times \frac{3}{7}$	$\frac{3}{4} \times \frac{3}{4}$	$5 \times \frac{2}{3}$	$4 \times \frac{2}{3}$
3.	$2 \times \frac{7}{16}$	$\frac{3}{8} \times 4$	$\frac{2}{5} \times 6$	$\frac{3}{4} \times 5$
4.	$2\frac{3}{4} \times 3$	$2\frac{7}{8} \times 6$	$3\frac{1}{3} \times 8$	$5 \times 2\frac{4}{5}$
5.	$3 \times 4\frac{5}{8}$	$5 \times 3\frac{2}{3}$	$2\frac{1}{5} \times 1\frac{1}{8}$	$1\frac{4}{7} \times 2\frac{3}{5}$
6.	$3\frac{1}{2} \times 3\frac{1}{3}$	$2\frac{2}{7} \times 2\frac{1}{8}$	$2\frac{1}{2} \times 4\frac{1}{4}$	$2\frac{3}{8} \times 1\frac{1}{2}$

Lesson 5.6 Problem Solving

SHOW YOUR WORK

Solve each problem. Write answers in simplest form.

1. Sam and José mowed $\frac{2}{3}$ of the yard. José mowed $\frac{3}{4}$ of that amount. What part of the yard did José mow?

   José mowed _____ of the yard.

2. Maria practices the piano $\frac{5}{6}$ of an hour every day. How many hours does she practice in 4 days?

   Maria practices _____ hours.

3. It takes 6 hours to clean the Smith's house. How long does it take to clean $\frac{5}{8}$ of the house?

   It takes _____ hours.

4. Raul can ride his bike $7\frac{1}{2}$ miles in one hour. How far can he ride in $2\frac{1}{3}$ hours?

   Raul can ride _____ miles.

5. If 8 boards are stacked on top of each other and each board is $2\frac{1}{4}$ inches thick, how high is the stack?

   The stack is _____ inches high.

6. A bag of potatoes weighs $2\frac{1}{2}$ pounds. How much would $3\frac{1}{3}$ bags weigh?

   The bags would weigh _____ pounds.

7. Jason put 6 pieces of chain together to make a fence. Each piece of chain was $3\frac{2}{5}$ feet long. How long was the chain?

   The chain was _____ feet long.

1.

2.

3.

4.

5.

6.

7.

Lesson 5.7 Reciprocals

The product of a number and its reciprocal is 1.
$\frac{3}{5}$ and $\frac{5}{3}$ are reciprocals.

$\frac{3}{5} \times \frac{5}{3} = \frac{15}{15} = 1$

The reciprocal of $\frac{3}{5}$ is $\frac{5}{3}$.

Find the reciprocal of a whole number by writing it as a fraction.

$4 = \frac{4}{1}$

The reciprocal of 4 is $\frac{1}{4}$.

Write the reciprocal.

	a	b	c	d	e	f
1.	$\frac{2}{3}$ ___	$\frac{5}{8}$ ___	$\frac{1}{4}$ ___	$\frac{3}{8}$ ___	$\frac{1}{6}$ ___	$\frac{3}{7}$ ___
2.	2 ___	3 ___	5 ___	9 ___	8 ___	5 ___
3.	7 ___	$\frac{7}{3}$ ___	$\frac{1}{3}$ ___	$\frac{1}{2}$ ___	$\frac{3}{4}$ ___	$\frac{1}{5}$ ___
4.	$\frac{4}{5}$ ___	$\frac{5}{6}$ ___	$\frac{1}{7}$ ___	$\frac{11}{8}$ ___	$\frac{6}{7}$ ___	$\frac{10}{3}$ ___
5.	$\frac{1}{9}$ ___	$\frac{11}{4}$ ___	$\frac{5}{9}$ ___	$\frac{4}{9}$ ___	$\frac{5}{2}$ ___	6 ___
6.	$\frac{7}{10}$ ___	$\frac{2}{5}$ ___	1 ___	$\frac{1}{15}$ ___	$\frac{7}{9}$ ___	$\frac{7}{16}$ ___
7.	$\frac{8}{9}$ ___	10 ___	$\frac{12}{7}$ ___	$\frac{15}{16}$ ___	$\frac{3}{2}$ ___	$\frac{5}{3}$ ___
8.	$\frac{9}{10}$ ___	$\frac{8}{11}$ ___	$\frac{2}{7}$ ___	4 ___	15 ___	$\frac{12}{11}$ ___
9.	12 ___	$\frac{6}{13}$ ___	$\frac{8}{3}$ ___	$\frac{14}{15}$ ___	$\frac{7}{13}$ ___	18 ___
10.	$\frac{3}{5}$ ___	$\frac{9}{16}$ ___	$\frac{5}{9}$ ___	$\frac{3}{10}$ ___	$\frac{4}{7}$ ___	$\frac{7}{16}$ ___

Lesson 5.8 Dividing Whole Numbers and Fractions

To divide, multiply by the reciprocal of the divisor.

divisor   reciprocal

$6 \div \frac{3}{8} = 6 \times \frac{8}{3}$

$= \frac{6}{1} \times \frac{8}{3}$

$= \frac{48}{3} = 16$

divisor   reciprocal

$\frac{4}{5} \div 8 = \frac{4}{5} \times \frac{1}{8}$

$= \frac{4}{40}$

$= \frac{1}{10}$

Divide. Write answers in simplest form.

	a	b	c	d
1.	$5 \div \frac{2}{3}$	$6 \div \frac{5}{8}$	$2 \div \frac{4}{5}$	$8 \div \frac{3}{7}$
2.	$9 \div \frac{3}{4}$	$10 \div \frac{5}{6}$	$15 \div \frac{3}{5}$	$4 \div \frac{7}{8}$
3.	$\frac{7}{8} \div 5$	$\frac{5}{8} \div 6$	$\frac{9}{10} \div 4$	$\frac{4}{5} \div 12$
4.	$\frac{4}{7} \div 7$	$\frac{5}{6} \div 8$	$\frac{5}{12} \div 5$	$\frac{2}{3} \div 4$

Lesson 5.9 Dividing Fractions by Fractions

To divide, multiply by the reciprocal of the divisor.

$$\frac{4}{5} \div \frac{8}{9} = \frac{4}{5} \times \frac{9}{8} = \frac{36}{40} = \frac{9}{10}$$

Divide. Write answers in simplest form.

	a	b	c	d
1.	$\frac{1}{2} \div \frac{3}{5}$	$\frac{3}{8} \div \frac{2}{3}$	$\frac{5}{8} \div \frac{3}{4}$	$\frac{2}{5} \div \frac{3}{8}$
2.	$\frac{1}{2} \div \frac{7}{8}$	$\frac{4}{5} \div \frac{3}{4}$	$\frac{5}{6} \div \frac{3}{8}$	$\frac{2}{3} \div \frac{4}{5}$
3.	$\frac{7}{8} \div \frac{1}{3}$	$\frac{7}{9} \div \frac{2}{3}$	$\frac{1}{3} \div \frac{2}{3}$	$\frac{5}{6} \div \frac{1}{3}$
4.	$\frac{3}{5} \div \frac{2}{3}$	$\frac{4}{9} \div \frac{3}{7}$	$\frac{1}{2} \div \frac{5}{8}$	$\frac{2}{3} \div \frac{7}{9}$

Lesson 5.10 Dividing Mixed Numbers

$3\frac{2}{5} \div 4$ Rename $3\frac{2}{5}$ as $\frac{17}{5}$. $4\frac{1}{3} \div 2\frac{3}{4}$

$\frac{17}{5} \div \frac{4}{1}$ Rename 4 as $\frac{4}{1}$. $\frac{13}{3} \div \frac{11}{4}$ Rename.

$\frac{17}{5} \times \frac{1}{4} = \frac{17}{20}$ Multiply by the reciprocal. $\frac{13}{3} \times \frac{4}{11} = \frac{52}{33} = 1\frac{19}{33}$ Multiply by the reciprocal.

Divide. Write answers in simplest form.

	a	b	c	d
1.	$2\frac{1}{2} \div 3\frac{1}{3}$	$1\frac{1}{8} \div 2\frac{1}{4}$	$8 \div 3\frac{1}{2}$	$2\frac{1}{3} \div 5$
2.	$4\frac{1}{2} \div 1\frac{1}{6}$	$4\frac{5}{6} \div 2\frac{2}{5}$	$4\frac{1}{3} \div 6$	$1\frac{1}{2} \div 3\frac{1}{8}$
3.	$6 \div 2\frac{1}{2}$	$1\frac{1}{2} \div 3$	$5 \div 3\frac{3}{4}$	$2\frac{1}{8} \div 3$
4.	$3\frac{3}{5} \div 4$	$3\frac{1}{3} \div 2\frac{3}{8}$	$1 \div 4\frac{1}{3}$	$9 \div 1\frac{2}{3}$

Lesson 5.11 Division Practice

Write the reciprocals.

	a	**b**	**c**	**d**
1.	$\frac{3}{4}$ _____	$\frac{11}{8}$ _____	3 _____	$\frac{2}{5}$ _____

Divide. Write answers in simplest form.

	a	**b**	**c**	**d**
2.	$2 \div \frac{3}{8}$	$4 \div \frac{2}{5}$	$6 \div \frac{4}{7}$	$3 \div \frac{7}{8}$
3.	$\frac{3}{4} \div \frac{1}{2}$	$\frac{4}{5} \div \frac{2}{3}$	$\frac{3}{8} \div \frac{7}{12}$	$\frac{4}{5} \div \frac{5}{6}$
4.	$5 \div 3\frac{1}{2}$	$2 \div 4\frac{1}{3}$	$6 \div 2\frac{2}{3}$	$7 \div 3\frac{1}{2}$
5.	$5\frac{2}{3} \div 4$	$3\frac{1}{8} \div 5$	$4\frac{3}{5} \div 6$	$1\frac{7}{8} \div 3$
6.	$3\frac{1}{2} \div 5\frac{2}{3}$	$4\frac{1}{3} \div 3\frac{1}{2}$	$2\frac{2}{3} \div 1\frac{3}{4}$	$1\frac{7}{8} \div 2\frac{1}{2}$

Lesson 5.12 Problem Solving

SHOW YOUR WORK

Solve each problem. Write answers in simplest form.

1. How many pieces of string that are $\frac{2}{7}$ of an inch long can be cut from a piece of string that is $\frac{7}{8}$ of an inch long?

   _____ pieces of string can be cut.

2. Five pounds of walnuts will be divided equally into containers which will hold $\frac{5}{8}$ of a pound each. How many containers will be filled?

   _____ containers will be filled.

3. A ribbon is $\frac{7}{9}$ of a yard long. It will be divided equally among 3 people. What is the length of ribbon that each person will get?

   Each person will get _____ of a yard.

4. A container holding $6\frac{2}{3}$ pints of juice will be divided equally among 5 people. How much juice will each person get?

   Each person will get _____ pints.

5. A 7-hour class will be divided into equal sessions of $1\frac{2}{5}$ hours. How many sessions will be needed?

   _____ sessions will be needed.

6. Jamie divided $6\frac{2}{5}$ ounces of candy into equal amounts. He put the candy into containers that hold $2\frac{2}{3}$ ounces each. How many containers will be filled?

   _____ containers will be filled.

1.
2.
3.
4.
5.
6.

Check What You Learned

Multiplying and Dividing Fractions

Multiply. Write answers in simplest form.

	a	**b**	**c**	**d**
1.	$\frac{2}{3} \times \frac{3}{4}$	$\frac{1}{2} \times \frac{3}{8}$	$\frac{7}{8} \times \frac{3}{5}$	$\frac{2}{7} \times \frac{5}{8}$
2.	$\frac{2}{3} \times 5$	$4 \times \frac{7}{8}$	$\frac{3}{5} \times 12$	$8 \times \frac{4}{7}$
3.	$3\frac{1}{8} \times 4$	$5 \times 7\frac{1}{2}$	$3\frac{2}{3} \times 6$	$10 \times 1\frac{2}{3}$
4.	$2\frac{1}{2} \times 3\frac{1}{3}$	$1\frac{1}{5} \times 3\frac{3}{4}$	$2\frac{1}{2} \times 2\frac{1}{2}$	$4\frac{1}{3} \times 2\frac{3}{5}$

Write the reciprocal.

5.	$\frac{3}{8}$ _____	5 _____	$\frac{12}{5}$ _____	$\frac{4}{7}$ _____

Divide. Write answers in simplest form.

6.	$5 \div \frac{2}{3}$	$\frac{4}{5} \div 5$	$7 \div \frac{3}{8}$	$\frac{7}{8} \div 2$
7.	$\frac{2}{3} \div \frac{4}{5}$	$\frac{7}{8} \div \frac{2}{3}$	$\frac{4}{7} \div \frac{3}{8}$	$\frac{5}{12} \div \frac{3}{4}$
8.	$3\frac{1}{8} \div 2\frac{1}{2}$	$4\frac{2}{3} \div 3\frac{1}{2}$	$2\frac{3}{4} \div 2\frac{3}{4}$	$1\frac{1}{2} \div 3\frac{1}{8}$

Check What You Learned

Multiplying and Dividing Fractions

Solve each problem. Write answers in simplest form.

9. Alice and Samantha watered $\frac{5}{6}$ of the yard together. Samantha watered $\frac{1}{3}$ of that amount. What part of the yard did Samantha water?

    Alice watered _____ of the yard.

10. Ramona sets aside $\frac{3}{4}$ of an hour for homework after school each day. How many hours does she do homework in 5 days?

    Ramona does _____ hours of homework in 5 days.

11. Anita can rollerblade $3\frac{1}{3}$ miles in 1 hour. How far can she rollerblade in $2\frac{1}{2}$ hours?

    Anita can rollerblade _____ miles.

12. A stack of 5 bricks is on the driveway. Each brick is $2\frac{1}{3}$ inches thick. How high is the stack of bricks?

    The stack of bricks is _____ inches high.

13. At the grocery, the bags of oranges weigh $4\frac{1}{3}$ pounds. How much would $2\frac{1}{2}$ bags of oranges weigh?
    The $2\frac{1}{2}$ bags would weigh _____ pounds.

14. It takes a baseball team 2 hours to complete a game. How long will it take to complete $\frac{2}{3}$ of the game?

    It will take _____ hours.

15. A bag holding $7\frac{1}{5}$ pounds of mixed nuts will be divided equally among 9 people. How many pounds of nuts will each person get?

    Each person will get _____ of a pound of nuts.

9.

10.

11.

12.

13.

14.

15.

Check What You Know

Adding and Subtracting Decimals

Change the fractions to decimals.

	a	**b**	**c**	**d**	**e**
1.	$\frac{2}{10}$ ____	$\frac{23}{100}$ ____	$\frac{2}{5}$ ____	$\frac{3}{4}$ ____	$\frac{49}{50}$ ____

Change the decimals to fractions or mixed numerals in simplest form.

2.   0.6 ____   0.08 ____   2.25 ____   3.15 ____   2.2 ____

Compare each pair of decimals using <, >, or =.

3.

a	**b**	**c**
6.203 ___ 6.214	2.4 ___ 2.400	48.28 ___ 46.281

Add or subtract.

	a	**b**	**c**	**d**
4.	46.83 21.25 + 3.64	732.84 +301.28	64.8 2.725 + 7.31	102.9 3.758 + 0.26
5.	78.625 −38.898	8.86 − 5.29	9.4 − 3.625	75.1 −23.021
6.	$28.75 +62.25	$4281.33 + 245.67	$75.52 2.57 + 1.88	$8.86 0.93 +2.42
7.	$72.58 −26.25	$50.00 −28.67	$3.28 − 2.79	$100.00 − 89.91

Check What You Know

Adding and Subtracting Decimals

CHAPTER 6 PRETEST

Solve each problem.

8. In a recent week, the rainfall was 0.2 inches for Monday, 0.7 inches for Tuesday, and 1.6 inches for Wednesday. What was the total amount of rainfall for those 3 days?

    The total amount of rainfall was _____ inches.

    Which day had the least amount of rainfall? _____

    Which day had the most rainfall? _____

    What was the difference between the highest and

    lowest amount of rainfall? _____ inches.

    Arrange the amounts of rainfall in order from least

    to greatest. _____

8.

9. Miranda wants to buy a tennis racket that costs $109.95. She has $68.50 saved from babysitting. How much more money does she need?

    Miranda needs _____.

9.

10. Julia went to the store and bought 3 items that cost $5.87, $21.62, and $11.48. What was the total cost of these 3 items?

    The total cost of the 3 items was _____.

10.

11. Joe wants to save $100 for basketball camp. He has $49.85. How much more money does he need?

    Joe needs _____.

11.

Lesson 6.1 Tenths and Hundredths

Numbers like 0.2, 3.4, 0.05, and 2.16 are called **decimals**.

$\frac{2}{10} = 0.2$ or two tenths

$\frac{5}{100} = 0.05$ or five hundredths

↑---- decimal point

$3\frac{4}{10} = 3.4$ or three and four tenths

$2\frac{16}{100} = 2.16$ or two and sixteen hundredths

Write each fraction or mixed numeral as a decimal.

	a	b	c	d
1.	$\frac{3}{10}$ _____	$\frac{1}{10}$ _____	$\frac{7}{100}$ _____	$\frac{4}{100}$ _____
2.	$2\frac{4}{10}$ _____	$7\frac{6}{10}$ _____	$21\frac{2}{100}$ _____	$58\frac{9}{100}$ _____

Write each decimal as a fraction or mixed numeral.

3.	0.4 _____	0.8 _____	0.06 _____	0.39 _____
4.	9.6 _____	13.3 _____	11.16 _____	689.05 _____

Write a decimal for each of the following.

	a	b
5.	nine tenths _____	eight hundredths _____
6.	five and two tenths _____	three and two hundredths _____
7.	one tenth _____	seventy-three hundredths _____

Write each decimal in words.

8. 2.7 _____

9. 0.62 _____

10. 5.08 _____

Lesson 6.2 Thousandths and Ten Thousandths

$\frac{3}{1000} = 0.003$ or three thousandths

$4\frac{23}{1000} = 4.023$ or four and twenty-three thousandths

$\frac{5}{10000} = 0.0005$ or five ten thousandths

$2\frac{53}{10000} = 2.0053$ or two and fifty-three ten thousandths

Write each fraction or mixed numeral as a decimal.

	a	b	c
1.	$\frac{7}{1000}$ _____	$\frac{25}{1000}$ _____	$\frac{561}{1000}$ _____
2.	$\frac{4}{10000}$ _____	$\frac{435}{10000}$ _____	$\frac{508}{10000}$ _____
3.	$2\frac{5}{1000}$ _____	$7\frac{861}{1000}$ _____	$4\frac{128}{1000}$ _____
4.	$5\frac{31}{10000}$ _____	$2\frac{165}{10000}$ _____	$8\frac{8}{10000}$ _____

Write each decimal as a fraction or mixed numeral.

5.	0.002 _____	0.089 _____	0.082 _____
6.	0.733 _____	0.4125 _____	0.0315 _____
7.	3.0201 _____	6.223 _____	4.301 _____
8.	25.1367 _____	3.1416 _____	7.2003 _____

Write a decimal for each of the following.

	a	b
9.	thirty-nine thousandths _____	eight and thirteen thousandths _____
10.	forty-nine ten thousandths _____	two and two hundred sixty-nine ten thousandths _____

Lesson 6.3 Changing Fractions to Decimals

Change $\frac{1}{5}$ to tenths.

$\frac{1}{5} = \frac{1 \times 2}{5 \times 2} = \frac{2}{10} = 0.2$

Change $\frac{1}{5}$ to hundredths.

$\frac{1}{5} = \frac{1 \times 20}{5 \times 20} = \frac{20}{100} = 0.20$

Change $\frac{1}{4}$ to hundredths.

$\frac{1}{4} = \frac{1 \times 25}{4 \times 25} = \frac{25}{100} = 0.25$

Change $\frac{1}{250}$ to thousandths.

$3\frac{1}{250} = 3\frac{1 \times 4}{250 \times 4} = 3\frac{4}{1000} = 3.004$

Change each of the following to a decimal as indicated.

	a	b	c
1.	Change $\frac{2}{5}$ to tenths.	Change $\frac{2}{5}$ to hundredths.	Change $\frac{2}{5}$ to thousandths.
2.	Change $3\frac{1}{2}$ to tenths.	Change $\frac{3}{25}$ to hundredths.	Change $\frac{17}{25}$ to thousandths.
3.	Change $2\frac{3}{5}$ to tenths.	Change $\frac{9}{20}$ to hundredths.	Change $\frac{29}{250}$ to thousandths.
4.	Change $2\frac{1}{5}$ to tenths.	Change $\frac{17}{50}$ to hundredths.	Change $1\frac{27}{100}$ to thousandths.
5.	Change $\frac{4}{5}$ to tenths.	Change $\frac{3}{4}$ to hundredths.	Change $\frac{3}{40}$ to thousandths.
6.	Change $7\frac{1}{2}$ to tenths.	Change $2\frac{3}{10}$ to hundredths.	Change $\frac{7}{125}$ to thousandths.

Lesson 6.4 Changing Decimals to Fractions

$0.4 = \frac{4}{10} = \frac{2}{5}$

$0.19 = \frac{19}{100}$

$2.35 = 2\frac{35}{100} = 2\frac{7}{20}$

$0.125 = \frac{125}{1000} = \frac{1}{8}$

$3.24 = 3\frac{24}{100} = 3\frac{6}{25}$

Write each decimal as a fraction or mixed numeral in simplest form.

	a	b	c	d
1.	0.4 _____	0.75 _____	3.1 _____	0.6 _____
2.	0.25 _____	1.3 _____	4.15 _____	2.2 _____
3.	3.127 _____	0.16 _____	8.4 _____	2.5 _____
4.	0.001 _____	0.04 _____	1.6 _____	1.01 _____
5.	0.64 _____	0.70 _____	4.6 _____	0.88 _____
6.	2.42 _____	0.56 _____	0.15 _____	0.002 _____
7.	2.3 _____	3.9 _____	1.95 _____	0.442 _____
8.	1.86 _____	3.31 _____	0.96 _____	0.12 _____
9.	4.76 _____	3.89 _____	4.08 _____	0.55 _____

Lesson 6.5 Comparing and Ordering Decimals

Which is larger: 4.2186 or 4.2225?

4.2<u>1</u>86

4.2<u>2</u>25

The ones are the same.
The tenths are the same.
The hundredths are different.

4.2186 < 4.2225

To order a group of decimals, line up the decimal points.

2.14, 2.08, 2.1, and 2.01

2.14   All the ones are the same. 2.14
2.08   and 2.1 have the same tenths digit,
2.1   but 4 is greater than zero. In the
2.01   other two, 8 is greater than 1.

List from least to greatest.
2.01, 2.08, 2.1, and 2.14

Compare each pair of decimals using <, >, or =.

	a		b		c	
1.	5.213	_____ 5.312	3.1	_____ 3.100	28.35	_____ 28.351
2.	6.32	_____ 6.032	5.17	_____ 5.172	144.3	_____ 144
3.	7.325	_____ 6.425	3.14	_____ 2.99	48.28	_____ 48.280
4.	0.2135	_____ 0.2233	1.006	_____ 1.060	0.010	_____ 0.001

Order the decimals from least to greatest.

5. 7.52, 7.498, 7.521, 7.6

    _____

6. 0.082, 0.080, 0.0823, 0.0088

    _____

7. 12.193, 12.201, 12.1931, 12.2001

    _____

8. 0.1164, 0.1084, 0.11639, 0.1171

    _____

Lesson 6.6 Adding Decimals

To add decimals, line up the decimal points. Then, add as you would whole numbers.

```
  1                 1               1
 26.2              4.65           0.086
+  5.3             0.08          +4.172
------            +7.34          ------
 31.5             -----          4.258
                  12.07
```

Add.

	a	b	c	d	e
1.	3.2 + 8.5	0.73 +0.88	1.84 +2.39	1.44 +8.37	4.23 +16.21
2.	0.014 +2.301	27.12 +13.09	42.325 + 2.014	6.54 +3.98	0.63 +5.72
3.	2.72 3.51 +4.22	68.52 1.72 + 0.55	27.15 105.21 + 2.63	7.2 8.8 +17.5	0.5 0.6 +21.2
4.	5.3 +2.8	68.68 + 8.48	32.132 +14.212	76.8 +24.3	1.119 +2.881
5.	6.50 +8.72	486.25 +103.88	168.42 + 35.69	25.093 + 3.112	14.001 + 2.883
6.	0.113 +0.658	4.211 +8.385	68.682 +25.529	2.004 +6.138	48.6 +53.9
7.	3.165 2.125 +1.612	0.018 0.403 +0.504	0.234 0.605 +0.721	4.005 2.903 +0.021	53.751 0.848 + 2.905

Lesson 6.7 Subtracting Decimals

To subtract decimals, line up the decimal points. Then, subtract as you would whole numbers.

```
  2 5.8        17.⁷⁴¹         ¹⁶ ¹³¹
-  1 1.3      - 1 5.3 3      X X.4 6 8
  1 4.5          2.0 8     -    8.5 7 3
                               8.8 9 5
```

Subtract.

	a	b	c	d	e
1.	0.8 − 0.3	2.6 − 1.8	3.7 − 1.8	0.96 − 0.27	1.9 − 0.4
2.	1 8.6 2 − 1 1.5 8	0.4 5 8 − 0.2 9 5	0.8 6 7 − 0.5 3 2	8.6 − 7.3	1 1.6 − 8.8
3.	4 3.6 − 2 7.3	1 5.3 2 − 1 4.9 5	0.6 5 − 0.3 2	2.6 9 5 − 0.1 2 8	8.0 4 − 0.9 3
4.	8.4 5 6 − 4.2 3 8	2 7.8 − 1 3.4	6 2.4 3 5 − 3 8.2 0 3	1 4.8 − 8.9	1 2.6 8 − 4.9 2
5.	1 9.6 − 2.8	1 8.5 0 7 − 9.3 6 2	5 4.8 2 − 2 8.6 6	7 6.8 − 3 5.1	1 8 8.4 − 9 3.1
6.	1 4.7 2 − 1 2.8 6	7.4 0 3 − 5.9 4 1	4.0 8 − 1.3 9	8.6 − 7.3	5.8 − 0.9
7.	8 8.4 − 1 9.2	4 8.6 6 3 − 1 2.2 0 5	9.9 2 − 4.3 8	7.4 − 3.7	2 1.2 5 − 1 5.0 8

Lesson 6.8 Inserting Zeros for Addition and Subtraction

You may insert 0s to help you add.

```
  0.6          1 1
  0.392      0.6 0 0
+ 1.23       0.392
            + 1.230
            ───────
             2.222
```

Insert 0s to help subtract.

```
  4.8          7 1
- 2.13       4.8 0
            - 2.13
            ──────
             2.67
```

Add or subtract.

	a	b	c	d	e
1.	2.1 + 0.259	0.48 + 1.1	12.1 + 3.26	49.76 + 3.1	5.992 + 3.25
2.	0.87 - 0.4	5.36 - 4.1	3.081 - 0.72	2.014 - 1.2	7.4 - 2.75
3.	14.37 + 3.002	26.3 + 5.25	8.81 + 0.135	5.63 + 2.1	6.317 + 5.8
4.	8.3 - 2.21	9.7 - 0.86	18.3 - 7.26	8.8 - 3.265	24.2 - 5.417
5.	4.72 + 8.5	0.6 + 0.423	0.92 + 4.083	8.3 + 0.613	2.57 + 8.803
6.	63.2 - 5.24	0.9 - 0.26	102.54 - 7.683	7. - 4.21	14.3 - 6.27
7.	1.832 4.34 + 6.2	6.742 8.331 + 0.2	26.14 - 8.092	14.1 - 8.092	0.08 - 0.013

Lesson 6.9 Adding Money

Add numerals representing money as you would decimals.

```
  1 1 1              1
$ 2 5 . 4 3      $ 4 . 0 8
+    5 . 9 8        0 . 2 5
_____      + 0 . 3 1
$ 3 1 . 4 1      _____
                 $ 4 . 6 4
```

Add.

	a	b	c	d	e
1.	$6.08 +0.12	$0.82 +3.61	$0.32 +0.89	$248.20 +435.89	$2.45 +9.33
2.	$480.25 + 63.48	$ 25.46 +108.20	$2643.25 +7284.68	$ 48.63 +193.20	$84.36 +39.02
3.	$95.59 + 8.22	$157.26 +388.45	$4922.78 +3144.65	$391.28 + 64.83	$1.59 +0.89
4.	$450.65 + 65.45	$751.62 +883.54	$2944.87 +4133.56	$45.92 +28.66	$7.63 +2.37
5.	$76.28 +31.31	$82.67 +13.13	$4186.30 + 25.00	$67.82 +37.73	$8.95 +7.77
6.	$6845.20 326.95 + 25.25	$1325.45 786.40 + 38.83	$69.98 21.32 + 7.60	$1.18 2.59 +0.99	$0.93 0.88 +0.76

Lesson 6.10 Subtracting Money

Subtract numerals representing money as you would decimals.

```
         1 9 9  9 1
 $ 7 8.6 5      $ 2̸0̸0̸.0̸0̸
 - 2 5.3 2      -   8 3.6 8
 ─────────      ───────────
 $ 5 3.3 3      $ 1 1 6.3 2
```

Subtract.

	a	**b**	**c**	**d**	**e**
1.	$95.59 − 8.22	$0.89 − 0.32	$10.00 − 3.72	$3.61 − .82	$9.33 −2.25
2.	$388.45 −157.26	$45.92 −28.66	$7.63 −2.37	$1.59 −0.89	$6.08 −0.12
3.	$435.89 −248.20	$480.25 − 63.48	$391.28 − 64.83	$67.82 −33.77	$108.20 − 52.64
4.	$326.95 − 52.25	$4923.65 −3144.78	$2.59 −1.18	$1325.45 − 768.40	$7284.68 −2643.25
5.	$76.28 −31.31	$0.93 −0.88	$3.69 −2.88	$193.20 − 48.63	$84.36 −39.02
6.	$100.00 − 65.83	$200.00 −108.92	$73.73 −67.82	$5.00 −2.87	$1000.00 − 273.18

Check What You Learned

Adding and Subtracting Decimals

Change the fractions to decimals.

	a	b	c	d	e
1.	$\frac{4}{10}$ ___	$\frac{37}{1000}$ ___	$\frac{1}{5}$ ___	$\frac{1}{4}$ ___	$\frac{23}{50}$ ___

Change the decimals to fractions or mixed numerals in simplest form.

2. 0.16 ___   0.95 ___   2.75 ___   3.5 ___   4.01 ___

Compare each pair of decimals using <, >, or =.

	a	b	c
3.	5.113 ___ 5.112	42.882 ___ 43.88	4.6 ___ 4.600

Add or subtract.

	a	b	c	d
4.	36.48 22.15 + 4.36	823.74 +308.81	72.3 5.272 + 3.17	109.2 5.738 + 0.62
5.	82.256 −39.888	6.88 − 2.95	8.4 −3.562	57.1 −32.012
6.	$58.25 +56.75	$3522.47 + 428.53	$24.67 2.88 + 1.93	$7.25 0.88 +1.38
7.	$62.58 −27.35	$70.00 −32.48	$3.32 − 2.87	$200.00 −187.02

Check What You Learned

Adding and Subtracting Decimals

Solve each problem.

8. For a craft project Alaina needs 5.7 inches of red ribbon, 8.3 inches of blue ribbon, and 4.9 inches of white ribbon. How many inches of ribbon does she need altogether?

Alaina needs _____ inches of ribbon.

Arrange the lengths of ribbon in order from shortest

to longest. _____

The color of the longest ribbon is _____.

The color of the shortest ribbon is _____.

What is the difference between the longest and

shortest lengths? _____ inches

9. Maurice wants to buy a pair of basketball shoes that are on sale for $64.95. He has $38.50 saved from his lawn mowing job. How much more money does he need?

Maurice needs _____.

10. Joanna went to the store and bought three items which cost $8.57, $12.26, and $14.81. What was the total cost of these three items?

The total cost of the 3 items was _____.

11. Ellen wants to go to soccer camp. The cost is $100. She has saved $53.75. How much more money does she need?

Ellen needs _____.

8.

9.

10.

11.

Mid-Test Chapters 1–6

Complete each problem as indicated.

	a	b	c	d	e

1.

a.
```
   834
 + 269
```

b.
```
  52648
   5795
+ 60159
```

c.
```
  6245
- 3105
```

d.
```
  73821
- 17608
```

e.
```
  89247
- 68879
```

2.

a.
```
  329
×   7
```

b.
```
  1843
×    5
```

c.
```
  432
×  57
```

d.
```
  2945
×  612
```

e.
```
  6281
×  408
```

3. 58)704   8)62472   45)6208   15)38725   68)29104

4.

a.
```
   6.4
 + 8.7
```

b.
```
  0.786
  0.41
+ 3.837
```

c.
```
 $67.52
+ 20.18
```

d.
```
 $16.52
-  6.93
```

e.
```
  27.63
-  6.397
```

Estimate.

5.

a.
```
  389
+ 527
```

b.
```
  784
- 328
```

c.
```
  876
×   6
```

d.
5)378

6.

a.
```
  6328
+ 4761
```

b.
```
  6735
- 2906
```

c.
```
  528
× 187
```

d.
7)4652

CHAPTERS 1–4 MID-TEST

Mid-Test Chapters 1–6

Change each fraction to a mixed numeral.

	a	b	c	d
7.	$\frac{7}{3}$	$\frac{8}{5}$	$\frac{10}{7}$	$\frac{23}{6}$

Change each mixed numeral to an improper fraction.

8.	$3\frac{1}{8}$	$5\frac{2}{5}$	$10\frac{2}{3}$	$6\frac{3}{4}$

Write the prime factorization of each number.

	a	b	c
9.	40	54	36

Multiply. Write answers in simplest form.

	a	b	c	d	e
10.	$\frac{2}{3} \times \frac{3}{4}$	$\frac{5}{6} \times \frac{7}{8}$	$6 \times \frac{5}{8}$	$2 \times 4\frac{2}{3}$	$3\frac{1}{3} \times 4\frac{1}{5}$

Find the least common multiple for each pair of numbers.

	a	b	c
11.	6 and 10	9 and 15	8 and 7

Mid-Test Chapters 1–6

Add, subtract, multiply, or divide. Write answers in simplest form.

	a	**b**	**c**	**d**	**e**
12.	$\frac{5}{6}$ $+\frac{1}{6}$	$\frac{3}{4}$ $+\frac{2}{3}$	$\frac{3}{8}$ $+\frac{5}{6}$	$4\frac{2}{3}$ $+3\frac{1}{4}$	$2\frac{1}{6}$ $+2\frac{1}{3}$
13.	$\frac{7}{8}$ $-\frac{5}{8}$	$\frac{5}{6}$ $-\frac{2}{3}$	6 $-\frac{3}{5}$	$5\frac{3}{4}$ $-2\frac{2}{3}$	$6\frac{1}{2}$ $-3\frac{5}{6}$
14.	$5 \div \frac{1}{6}$	$\frac{3}{5} \div 4$	$\frac{7}{8} \div \frac{2}{3}$	$4\frac{1}{3} \div 5$	$3\frac{1}{8} \div 1\frac{2}{3}$

Change each of the following to a decimal as indicated.

	a	**b**	**c**
15.	$2\frac{1}{2}$ to tenths	$2\frac{1}{2}$ to hundredths	$2\frac{1}{2}$ to thousandths
	_____	_____	_____

Change each decimal to a fraction or mixed numeral in simplest form.

16.   0.38 _____   0.08 _____   0.012 _____

17.   2.14 _____   3.9 _____   154.083 _____

Mid-Test Chapters 1–6

CHAPTERS 1–4 MID-TEST

18. The attendance at a school festival was 786 on Friday night, 908 on Saturday, and 812 on Sunday. What was the total attendance?

The total attendance was _____.

18.

19. The distance from Atlanta, Georgia, to Boise, Idaho, is 2,214 miles. The distance from Atlanta, Georgia, to Houston, Texas is 789 miles. How much farther is it from Atlanta to Boise than from Atlanta to Houston?

It is _____ miles farther.

19.

20. Marcia has $\frac{7}{8}$ of a pound of candy. She gives $\frac{2}{5}$ of the candy to Lucinda. How much candy does Lucinda get?

Lucinda gets _____ of candy.

20.

21. A board is $7\frac{2}{3}$ feet long. A piece $4\frac{5}{8}$ feet long is cut off. What is the length of the rest of the board?

The length of the rest of the board is _____ feet.

21.

22. Inez went to the store and bought three items that cost $19.65, $27.35, and $20.38. What was the total cost of these three items?

The total cost of the three items was _____.

22.

23. A brick paving stone is 13 centimeters thick. How high is a stack of 89 paving stones?

The stack is _____ centimeters high.

23.

Check What You Know

Multiplying and Dividing Decimals

Multiply or divide.

	a	b	c	d
1.	2.86 × 0.3	238.2 × 3.6	3.152 × 13	0.82 × 0.43
2.	$35.26 × 32	$78.53 × 16	0.652 × 100	0.0037 × 10
3.	3.21 × 8.72	0.598 × 5.37	0.0032 × 0.42	74.6 × 0.033

Divide and check by multiplying.

4. 7)39.9   5)61.65   0.08)64   0.3)726

5. 0.6)0.036   0.05)37.5   0.83)2.1995   3.8)0.019

6. 14)$7.70   18)$102.24   0.056)9.8   3.4)0.085

Check What You Know

SHOW YOUR WORK

Multiplying and Dividing Decimals

Solve each problem.

7. A box of nails weighs 0.4 pound. How much do 42 boxes of nails weigh?

The boxes weigh _____ pounds.

7.

8. A floor tile is 0.75 feet wide. How many feet can you cover with 28 tiles?

The area covered is _____ wide.

8.

9. A carton of bolts weighs 7.8 pounds. How much does a carton containing 0.38 times as many bolts weigh?

The carton weighs _____ pounds.

9.

10. Fifty-two bags of popcorn cost $136.76. How much does one bag cost?

One bag costs _____.

10.

11. One bag of peanuts costs $1.52. How many bags can you buy with $34.96?

You can buy _____ bags.

11.

12. A box containing 78.4 pounds of coffee will be divided into containers that hold 0.56 pound each. How many containers can be filled?

_____ containers can be filled.

12.

Lesson 7.1 Multiplying Decimals

The number of digits to the right of the decimal point in the product is the sum of the number of digits to the right of the decimal point of the factors.

```
        0.4              0.28                3.2 4 3 2
     ×  0.2           ×   0.6             ×       0.1 3
     ───────          ────────            ──────────────
        0.0 8            0.1 6 8               9 7 2 9 6
                                          +  3 2 4 3 2
If needed, add zeros as place holders.    ──────────────
                                          0.4 2 1 6 1 6
```

Multiply.

	a	b	c	d	e
1.	0.7 × 8	0.08 × 0.5	0.3 2 5 × 0.3	1.6 8 × 8	25 × 0.7
2.	0.03 × 3.06	0.1 6 2 × 0.3	8.0 3 × 3.5	0.2 9 7 × 7.1	7 6.4 × 3.6
3.	5 3.6 4 × 0.3 7	3 2 8.1 × 0.6 3	9.8 0 6 × 3 1	6 0 0.3 × 0.0 3 4	8 9 5 × 0.6 3
4.	2 7.1 × 3.5 4	3.2 6 3 × 1 8	1.2 5 3 × 1 2	5 8.9 × 0.0 3 8	0.8 2 × 0.8 2
5.	0.2 8 3 × 0.6	0.1 7 8 × 5 3	0.8 3 × 0.2 3	3.6 × 0.0 2 5	4 8.2 × 0.2 6

Lesson 7.2 Multiplying Money

$$
\begin{array}{r}
\$0.08 \\
\times\ 16 \\
\hline
48 \\
+\ 8 \\
\hline
\$1.28
\end{array}
\qquad
\begin{array}{r}
\$25.63 \\
\times\ 25 \\
\hline
12815 \\
+5126 \\
\hline
\$640.75
\end{array}
$$

Multiply.

	a	b	c	d

1.

$$
\begin{array}{r}\$0.82\\ \times\ 7\\ \hline\end{array}
\qquad
\begin{array}{r}\$0.09\\ \times\ 17\\ \hline\end{array}
\qquad
\begin{array}{r}\$0.48\\ \times\ 22\\ \hline\end{array}
\qquad
\begin{array}{r}\$0.77\\ \times\ 38\\ \hline\end{array}
$$

2.

$$
\begin{array}{r}\$3.78\\ \times\ 183\\ \hline\end{array}
\qquad
\begin{array}{r}\$9.67\\ \times\ 252\\ \hline\end{array}
\qquad
\begin{array}{r}\$6.85\\ \times\ 75\\ \hline\end{array}
\qquad
\begin{array}{r}\$2.23\\ \times\ 118\\ \hline\end{array}
$$

3.

$$
\begin{array}{r}\$25.63\\ \times\ 21\\ \hline\end{array}
\qquad
\begin{array}{r}\$48.45\\ \times\ 9\\ \hline\end{array}
\qquad
\begin{array}{r}\$87.35\\ \times\ 13\\ \hline\end{array}
\qquad
\begin{array}{r}\$54.33\\ \times\ 41\\ \hline\end{array}
$$

4.

$$
\begin{array}{r}\$175.50\\ \times\ 8\\ \hline\end{array}
\qquad
\begin{array}{r}\$343.08\\ \times\ 15\\ \hline\end{array}
\qquad
\begin{array}{r}\$488.62\\ \times\ 9\\ \hline\end{array}
\qquad
\begin{array}{r}\$500.62\\ \times\ 12\\ \hline\end{array}
$$

5.

$$
\begin{array}{r}\$88.66\\ \times\ 17\\ \hline\end{array}
\qquad
\begin{array}{r}\$286.22\\ \times\ 40\\ \hline\end{array}
\qquad
\begin{array}{r}\$150.65\\ \times\ 6\\ \hline\end{array}
\qquad
\begin{array}{r}\$29.33\\ \times\ 111\\ \hline\end{array}
$$

Lesson 7.3 Multiplication Practice

3.62 × 10 ‾‾‾‾‾ 36.20 or 36.2	3.62 × 100 ‾‾‾‾‾ 362.00 or 362	3.62 × 1000 ‾‾‾‾‾ 3620.00 or 3620	Shortcut: $3.62 \times 10 = 36.2$ $3.62 \times 100 = 362$ $3.620 \times 1000 = 3620$

Multiply.

	a	b	c	d	e
1.	6.542 × 10	0.425 × 100	2.645 × 10	5.264 × 1000	0.0632 × 100
2.	10.64 × 100	106.4 × 10	64.01 × 1000	0.0003 × 1000	0.0062 × 100
3.	0.025 × 10	0.632 × 1000	2.593 × 1000	93.25 × 10	72.45 × 100
4.	32 × 100	0.0023 × 10	27.62 × 1000	0.183 × 100	0.318 × 1000
5.	0.2113 × 100	0.1213 × 1000	0.3211 × 10	2.339 × 100	3.239 × 1000

Lesson 7.3 Multiplication Practice

Multiply.

	a	b	c	d
	2.53	0.73	0.008	0.419
1.	× 21.2	× 0.25	× 0.016	× 35
	8.03	8.904	213.8	400.8
2.	× 5.3	× 32	× 0.23	× 0.034
	6.31	30.6	0.859	0.62
3.	× 5.43	× 3.41	× 37.5	× 0.53
	$12.86	$98.99	$0.88	$38.44
4.	× 22	× 6	× 19	× 17
	7.21	0.0025	0.03	67.4
5.	× 3.82	× 0.36	× 0.07	× 0.031
	86.3	217.4	0.23	276.3
6.	× 0.31	× 81	× 0.45	× 0.44

Lesson 7.4 Problem Solving

SHOW YOUR WORK

Solve each problem.

1. A package weighs 2.6 pounds. How much do 8 of the same-sized packages weigh?

   The packages weigh _____ pounds.

2. A paving stone is 0.625 inch thick. How thick is a stack of 37 paving stones?

   The stack is _____ inches thick.

3. Prizes for a carnival booth cost $0.37 each. How much do 1,000 prizes cost?

   The prizes cost _____.

4. Mrs. Anderson bought party favors for the 24 students in her class. Each favor costs $2.27. How much did all the party favors cost?

   The favors cost _____.

5. A box of grass seed weighs 0.62 pound. How much does a box containing 0.75 times as much grass seed weigh?

   The box weighs _____ pound.

6. A sheet of plastic wrap is 0.013 inch thick. How thick is a stack of 27 sheets of that same wrap?

   The stack is _____ inch thick.

| 1. |
| 2. |
| 3. |
| 4. |
| 5. |
| 6. |

Lesson 7.5 Dividing Decimals by Whole Numbers

Place a decimal point in the quotient directly above the decimal point in the dividend. Divide as if both were whole numbers.

```
      0.2
   8)1.6
    -16
```

```
     0.015
   7)0.105
    - 7
        35
```

```
     .121
   6).726
    -6
      12
     -12
       06
```

```
     .6253
   5)3.1265
    -30
       12
      -10
        26
       -25
         15
```

Divide.

	a	b	c	d

1. 6)46.2   7)3.43   5)1.025   8)1.384

2. 9)8.181   7)2.877   3)15.024   7)2.058

3. 6)3.72   3)0.0174   4)9.88   5)28.25

4. 9)16.83   5)0.1875   6)4.68   4)24.8

Lesson 7.6 Dividing Whole Numbers by Decimals

Multiply the divisor and dividend by 10, by 100, or by 1000 so the new divisor is a whole number.

$$0.8 \overline{)72.0} = 8 \overline{)720}$$
Multiply by 10.

$$\begin{array}{r} 90 \\ 8\overline{)720} \\ -720 \\ \hline \end{array}$$

$$.04 \overline{)34.00} = 4 \overline{)3400}$$
Multiply by 100.

$$\begin{array}{r} 850 \\ 4\overline{)3400} \\ -32 \\ \hline 20 \\ -20 \\ \hline 0 \end{array}$$

$$0.003 \overline{)27.000} = 3 \overline{)27000}$$
Multiply by 1000.

$$\begin{array}{r} 9000 \\ 3\overline{)27000} \\ -27000 \\ \hline \end{array}$$

Divide.

	a	b	c	d
1.	$0.8\overline{)48}$	$0.4\overline{)80}$	$0.6\overline{)216}$	$0.5\overline{)21}$
2.	$0.07\overline{)28}$	$0.02\overline{)45}$	$0.08\overline{)24}$	$0.03\overline{)15}$
3.	$0.006\overline{)54}$	$0.007\overline{)14}$	$0.008\overline{)72}$	$0.003\overline{)282}$
4.	$0.7\overline{)3283}$	$0.06\overline{)2724}$	$0.004\overline{)12}$	$0.9\overline{)891}$

Lesson 7.7 Dividing Decimals by Decimals

Multiply the divisor and dividend by 10, by 100, or by 1000 so the new divisor is a whole number.

$$0.3\overline{)1.17} = 3\overline{)11.7}$$
Multiply
by 10.

$$\begin{array}{r} 3.9 \\ 3\overline{)11.7} \\ -9 \\ \hline 27 \end{array}$$

$$0.05\overline{)7.50} = 5\overline{)750}$$
Multiply
by 100.

$$\begin{array}{r} 150 \\ 5\overline{)750} \\ -5 \\ \hline 25 \\ -25 \\ \hline 0 \end{array}$$

$$0.002\overline{)3.600} = 2\overline{)3600}$$

$$\begin{array}{r} 1800 \\ 2\overline{)3600} \end{array}$$

Divide.

	a	b	c	d
1.	$0.8\overline{)0.168}$	$0.03\overline{)1.68}$	$0.004\overline{)0.012}$	$0.5\overline{)25.5}$
2.	$0.06\overline{)2.16}$	$0.07\overline{)0.245}$	$0.009\overline{)37.8}$	$0.7\overline{)17.206}$
3.	$0.3\overline{)0.027}$	$0.06\overline{)27.12}$	$0.008\overline{)4}$	$0.5\overline{)0.8}$
4.	$.002\overline{)45}$	$0.07\overline{)50.4}$	$0.6\overline{)0.0192}$	$0.04\overline{)1.92}$

Lesson 7.8 Dividing by Two Digits

Multiply the divisor and dividend by 10, by 100, or by 1000 so the divisor is a whole number.

$$3.5\overline{)140} = 35\overline{)140}$$
Multiply by 10.
$$\begin{array}{r} 4 \\ 35\overline{)140} \\ -140 \end{array}$$

$$0.42\overline{)16.80} = 42\overline{)1680}$$
Multiply by 100.
$$\begin{array}{r} 40 \\ 42\overline{)1680} \\ -168 \\ \hline 0 \end{array}$$

$$0.027\overline{)8.100} = 27\overline{)8100}$$
Multiply by 1000.
$$\begin{array}{r} 300 \\ 27\overline{)8100} \\ -8100 \end{array}$$

Divide.

	a	b	c	d
1.	$2.3\overline{)5.06}$	$3.4\overline{)289}$	$5.2\overline{)2.08}$	$7.2\overline{)10.8}$
2.	$0.45\overline{)18}$	$0.22\overline{)1.166}$	$0.63\overline{)25.2}$	$0.98\overline{)63.7}$
3.	$0.032\overline{)96}$	$0.015\overline{)0.45}$	$0.068\overline{)0.017}$	$0.012\overline{)0.0144}$
4.	$2.4\overline{)0.96}$	$0.62\overline{)24.8}$	$0.016\overline{)0.08}$	$0.85\overline{)5.1}$

Lesson 7.9 Dividing Money

```
        $ 6.12              $6.40  ←----           $0.17
    4)$ 2 4.4 8      2 2)$ 1 4 0.8 0           5)$ 0.8 5
      - 2 4               - 1 3 2                 - 5
          0 4                   8 8                 3 5
        -   4                 - 8 8               - 3 5
            0 8                     0                   0
          -   8
```

Zero is necessary to
indicate 40 cents.

Divide.

	a	b	c	d
1.	6)$50.70	7)$365.61	5)$263.80	4)$180.00
2.	24)$141.12	42)$359.10	23)$0.69	4)$0.92
3.	14)$54.04	54)$2160.00	32)$8.00	7)$56
4.	28)$700	55)$110.00	28)$98.00	14)$0.70
5.	12)$6014.40	18)$270.00	24)$54.00	75)$1.50

Lesson 7.10 Division Practice

To check division problems, multiply the divisor by the quotient. The product should be the same as the dividend.

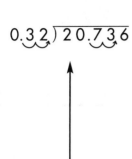

$$32)\overline{2073.6} \quad \begin{array}{r} 64.8 \\ \hline 2073.6 \\ -192 \\ \hline 153 \\ -128 \\ \hline 256 \\ -256 \\ \hline 0 \end{array}$$

$$\begin{array}{r} 64.8 \\ \times\ 0.32 \\ \hline 1296 \\ +1944 \\ \hline 20.736 \end{array}$$

Divide and check by multiplying.

a	b	c

1. $7)\overline{\$379.40}$ $7)\overline{\$61.25}$ $3)\overline{\$37.50}$

2. $0.6)\overline{48}$ $0.05)\overline{26}$ $0.006)\overline{84}$

3. $0.4)\overline{0.056}$ $0.03)\overline{0.93}$ $0.007)\overline{0.091}$

4. $0.46)\overline{2.668}$ $0.065)\overline{9.1}$ $3.8)\overline{0.095}$

Lesson 7.11 Problem Solving

Solve each problem.

1. A car travels 12 miles on 0.3 gallon of gas. How far can it travel on 1 gallon?

   The car can travel _____ miles.

1.

2. A box containing 48 pounds of coffee will be divided into packages that each hold 0.8 pound. How many packages are needed?

   _____ packages are needed.

2.

3. It takes Maxine 0.3 hour to make a potholder. How many potholders can she make in 4.5 hours?

   She can make _____ potholders.

3.

4. A stack of bricks is 38 inches high. Each brick is 1.52 inches high. How many bricks are in the stack?

   _____ bricks are in the stack.

4.

5. A collection of nickels is worth $18.60. How many nickels are in the collection?

   _____ nickels are in the collection.

5.

6. Each prize for a carnival booth costs $0.32. How many prizes can you buy with $96?

   You can buy _____ prizes.

6.

Check What You Learned

Multiplying and Dividing Decimals

Multiply or divide.

	a	**b**	**c**	**d**
1.	4.39 × 0.8	365.3 × 5.2	2.235 × 16	0.76 × 0.53
2.	$28.73 × 42	$67.45 × 23	0.312 × 10	0.0026 × 100
3.	4.26 × 7.62	0.926 × 6.47	0.0038 × 0.42	86.3 × 0.043

Divide and check by multiplying.

4. $8\overline{)53.6}$ $7\overline{)79.31}$ $0.6\overline{)78}$ $0.09\overline{)738}$

5. $0.8\overline{)0.096}$ $0.07\overline{)50.4}$ $0.79\overline{)2.5596}$ $4.6\overline{)0.023}$

6. $18\overline{)\$13.50}$ $23\overline{)\$129.26}$ $0.048\overline{)2.4}$ $5.6\overline{)0.196}$

Check What You Learned

SHOW YOUR WORK

Multiplying and Dividing Decimals

Solve each problem.

7. A can of coffee weighs 0.55 pound. How much do 45 cans of coffee weigh?

The cans of coffee weigh _____ pounds.

7.

8. A floor tile is 1.1 feet wide. What area can you cover with 32 tiles of the same size?

The area you can cover is _____
feet wide.

8.

9. A bag of wood chips weighs 12.4 pounds. How much does a bag containing 0.42 times as many wood chips weigh?

The bag weighs _____ pounds.

9.

10. Forty-seven candy bars cost $88.36. How much does one candy bar cost?

The candy bar costs _____.

10.

11. One comic book costs $2.23. How many comic books can you buy for $71.36?

You can buy _____ comic books.

11.

12. A box holding 80.6 pounds of nails will be divided into containers that hold 0.62 pound each. How many containers can be filled?

_____ containers can be filled.

12.

Check What You Know

Finding Percents

Change the following fractions and decimals to percents.

a	b	c
1. $\frac{6}{100}$ = _____	$\frac{3}{10}$ = _____	$\frac{2}{5}$ = _____
2. $\frac{11}{20}$ = _____	$\frac{7}{25}$ = _____	$\frac{13}{50}$ = _____
3. 0.08 = _____	0.7 = _____	0.32 = _____
4. 0.182 = _____	2.25 = _____	0.75 = _____

Change each percent to a decimal.

5. 12% = _____	65% = _____	36% = _____
6. 5.75% = _____	150% = _____	0.1% = _____

Change each percent to a fraction in simplest form.

7. 35% = _____	52% = _____	16% = _____
8. 75% = _____	80% = _____	55% = _____

Complete the following.

9. 10% of 12 = _____	23% of 38 = _____	42% of 25 = _____
10. 72% of 8 = _____	17% of 86 = _____	110% of 20 = _____
11. 59% of 6 = _____	50% of 21 = _____	300% of 8 = _____
12. 40% of 2 = _____	2% of 112 = _____	98% of 68 = _____

NAME _____

Check What You Know

Finding Percents

Solve each problem.

13. At East Side Middle School, $\frac{3}{4}$ of the students ride the bus to school. What percent of the students ride the bus?

    _____ of the students ride the bus.

    13.

14. Morgan got $\frac{17}{20}$ of the questions on a science test correct. What percent of the questions did she get correct?

    Morgan got _____ percent of the questions correct.

    14.

15. The band at East Side Middle School lost 20 percent of its 230 members from last year. How many band members left?

    _____ band members left.

    15.

16. A sweater is on sale for 40 percent off its original price of $29.95. What is the amount of savings?

    The savings is _____.

    16.

17. A 25-pound mixture of cashews and peanuts contains 65 percent peanuts by weight. How many pounds of peanuts are in the mixture?

    There are _____ pounds of peanuts in the mixture.

    17.

18. There are 1,560 students at West Side Middle School. Three fourths of the students bring their lunch to school. How many students bring their lunch?

    _____ students bring their lunch.

    18.

Lesson 8.1 Understanding Percents

The symbol **%** (percent) means $\frac{1}{100}$ or 0.01 (one hundredth).

$7\% = 7 \times \frac{1}{100}$ $6\% = 6 \times 0.01$ $23\% = 23 \times \frac{1}{100}$ $47\% = 47 \times 0.01$

     $= \frac{7}{1} \times \frac{1}{100}$ $= 0.06$ $= \frac{23}{100}$ $= 0.47$

     $= \frac{7}{100}$

Write the fraction or decimal for each percent. Write fractions in simplest form.

	Percent	Fraction	Decimal
1.	2%	_____	_____
2.	8%	_____	_____
3.	27%	_____	_____
4.	13%	_____	_____
5.	68%	_____	_____
6.	72%	_____	_____
7.	56%	_____	_____
8.	11%	_____	_____
9.	3%	_____	_____
10.	22%	_____	_____
11.	17%	_____	_____
12.	83%	_____	_____
13.	97%	_____	_____
14.	43%	_____	_____

Lesson 8.2 Percent to Fraction and Fraction to Percent

Percent to Fraction	Fraction to Percent	Mixed Numeral
$40\% = 40 \times \frac{1}{100}$	$\frac{1}{4} = \frac{1 \times 25}{4 \times 25}$	$2\frac{1}{5} = \frac{11}{5}$
$= \frac{40}{1} \times \frac{1}{100}$	$= \frac{25}{100} = 25\%$	$\frac{11 \times 20}{5 \times 20} = \frac{220}{100}$
$= \frac{40}{100} = \frac{2 \times 20}{5 \times 20}$	Rename fraction with 100 as the denominator.	$2\frac{1}{5} = 220\%$
$= \frac{2}{5}$		

Write the percents as fractions in simplest form and the fractions and mixed numerals as percents.

	a	b	c	d
1.	$30\% =$ _____	$\frac{9}{20} =$ _____	$19\% =$ _____	$\frac{13}{50} =$ _____
2.	$\frac{3}{4} =$ _____	$32\% =$ _____	$\frac{4}{5} =$ _____	$48\% =$ _____
3.	$1\frac{1}{2} =$ _____	$44\% =$ _____	$\frac{13}{20} =$ _____	$56\% =$ _____
4.	$110\% =$ _____	$1\frac{3}{4} =$ _____	$68\% =$ _____	$\frac{19}{20} =$ _____
5.	$\frac{3}{5} =$ _____	$5\% =$ _____	$\frac{13}{25} =$ _____	$74\% =$ _____
6.	$57\% =$ _____	$\frac{7}{50} =$ _____	$12\% =$ _____	$\frac{19}{25} =$ _____
7.	$6\% =$ _____	$\frac{7}{10} =$ _____	$38\% =$ _____	$1\frac{2}{25} =$ _____
8.	$\frac{9}{10} =$ _____	$72\% =$ _____	$\frac{27}{50} =$ _____	$160\% =$ _____
9.	$85\% =$ _____	$\frac{1}{10} =$ _____	$73\% =$ _____	$39\% =$ _____
10.	$\frac{1}{5} =$ _____	$84\% =$ _____	$\frac{23}{20} =$ _____	$\frac{7}{20} =$ _____
11.	$35\% =$ _____	$\frac{3}{10} =$ _____	$58\% =$ _____	$4\% =$ _____
12.	$1\frac{1}{4} =$ _____	$140\% =$ _____	$1\frac{3}{10} =$ _____	$\frac{7}{25} =$ _____

Lesson 8.3 Percent to Decimal and Decimal to Percent

Percent to Decimal
$25\% = 25 \times 0.01 = 0.25$
$3.4\% = 3.4 \times 0.01 = 0.034$
$12\% = 12 \times 0.01 = 0.12$

Notice that the decimal point
is moved 2 places to the left
when you multiply by 0.01.

Decimal to Percent
Rename the decimal as a fraction
with a denominator of 100.
$0.73 = \frac{0.73}{1} = \frac{0.73 \times 100}{100} = \frac{73}{100}$
$= 73\%$

$0.0625 = \frac{0.0625 \times 100}{1 \times 100}$
$= \frac{6.25}{100} = 6.25\%$

Write the percents as decimals and the decimals as percents.

	a	b	c
1.	4% = _____	3.5 = _____	16.5% = _____
2.	0.51 = _____	0.6% = _____	0.345 = _____
3.	33% = _____	0.025 = _____	15% = _____
4.	0.08 = _____	125% = _____	0.63 = _____
5.	0.75 = _____	88% = _____	0.478 = _____
6.	98% = _____	0.125 = _____	4.5% = _____
7.	0.7 = _____	21% = _____	0.23 = _____
8.	3.5% = _____	0.45 = _____	73.5% = _____
9.	0.29 = _____	0.3 = _____	1% = _____
10.	101% = _____	200% = _____	0.06 = _____
11.	0.625 = _____	64% = _____	1.15% = _____
12.	57% = _____	0.85 = _____	0.425 = _____

Lesson 8.4 Multiplying by Fractions

$35\% \text{ of } 60 = 35\% \times 60$

$\quad = \frac{35}{100} \times 60$

$\quad = \frac{7}{20} \times \frac{60}{1} = \frac{420}{20} = \frac{42}{2}$

$\quad = 21$

$40\% \text{ of } 32 =$

$40\% \times 32 = \frac{40}{100} \times \frac{32}{1}$

$\quad = \frac{2}{5} \times \frac{32}{1} = \frac{64}{5}$

$\quad = 12\frac{4}{5}$

Write each answer in simplest form.

	a	b
1.	8% of 65 = _____	95% of 80 = _____
2.	30% of 32 = _____	25% of 28 = _____
3.	150% of 12 = _____	25% of 30 = _____
4.	28% of 7 = _____	10% of 38 = _____
5.	40% of 20 = _____	15% of 45 = _____
6.	80% of 80 = _____	20% of 75 = _____
7.	45% of 70 = _____	18% of 45 = _____
8.	4% of 92 = _____	16% of 90 = _____
9.	90% of 60 = _____	25% of 86 = _____
10.	12% of 40 = _____	9% of 60 = _____
11.	60% of 60 = _____	95% of 20 = _____
12.	21% of 50 = _____	3% of 25 = _____

Lesson 8.5 Multiplying by Decimals

26% of 73.2 $26\% = 26 \times 0.01 = 0.26$

$$
\begin{array}{r}
7\,3.2 \\
\times\quad 0.2\,6 \\
\hline
4\,3\,9\,2 \\
+\;1\,4\,6\,4 \\
\hline
1\,9.0\,3\,2
\end{array}
$$

26% of 73.2 = 19.032

Complete the following.

	a	**b**
1.	32% of 64 = _____	26% of 40 = _____
2.	2.5% of 89 = _____	1.2% of 385 = _____
3.	58% of 12 = _____	250% of 8 = _____
4.	73% of 8.4 = _____	49% of 86 = _____
5.	0.8% of 256 = _____	11% of 29 = _____
6.	120% of 35 = _____	7.5% of 60 = _____
7.	84% of 7 = _____	40% of 95 = _____
8.	20% of 45 = _____	22% of 142 = _____
9.	9.2% of 63 = _____	80% of 80 = _____
10.	7% of 112 = _____	62% of 45 = _____
11.	16% of 16 = _____	12% of 200 = _____
12.	1.8% of 240 = _____	18% of 15 = _____

Lesson 8.6 Problem Solving

SHOW YOUR WORK

Solve each problem.

1. The sales tax on the purchase of a refrigerator that costs $695 is 7 percent. What is the amount of sales tax?

   The sales tax is _____.

2. A stove that costs $695 will be on sale next week for 28 percent off its regular price. What is the amount of savings?

   The savings will be _____.

3. In math class, 60 percent of the students are males. There are 30 students in the class. How many students are males?

   There are _____ males.

4. East Side Middle School has 1,500 students. Thirty-two percent of them are in sixth grade. How many sixth-grade students are there?

   There are _____ sixth-grade students.

5. Lauren is saving for gymnastics camp. Camp costs $225 to attend. She has 40 percent of the money saved. How much money has she saved?

   Lauren has saved _____.

6. Of the 1,500 students attending East Side Middle School, twenty-five percent are running for student council. How many students are running for student council?

   _____ students are running for student council.

1.
2.
3.
4.
5.
6.

Check What You Learned

Finding Percents

Change the following fractions and decimals to percents.

	a	b	c

1. $\frac{13}{100} =$ _____ $\frac{7}{10} =$ _____ $\frac{4}{5} =$ _____

2. $\frac{9}{20} =$ _____ $\frac{11}{25} =$ _____ $\frac{39}{50} =$ _____

3. 0.02 = _____   0.9 = _____   0.23 = _____

4. 1.82 = _____   0.0225 = _____   0.25 = _____

Change each percent to a decimal.

5. 23% = _____   85% = _____   175% = _____

6. 1.25% = _____   3% = _____   0.6% = _____

Change each percent to a fraction in simplest form.

7. 55% = _____   56% = _____   24% = _____

8. 60% = _____   25% = _____   85% = _____

Complete the following.

9. 20% of 7 = _____   33% of 28 = _____   52% of 42 = _____

10. 82% of 6 = _____   87% of 16 = _____   130% of 30 = _____

11. 69% of 8 = _____   50% of 33 = _____   400% of 9 = _____

12. 60% of 3 = _____   3% of 117 = _____   96% of 88 = _____

Check What You Learned

SHOW YOUR WORK

Finding Percents

Solve each problem.

13. In Keon's homeroom class, $\frac{3}{5}$ of the students participate in sports. What percent of students participate in sports?

_____ percent participate in sports.

13.

---

14. Fifty-five percent of the students at West Side Middle School walk to school. What fraction of the students walk to school?

_____ of the students walk to school.

14.

---

15. A new car that costs $17,500 loses 25 percent of its value in the first year. How much is the loss of value?

The loss of value is _____.

15.

---

16. The 140-member chorus at West Side Middle School wants to add 30 percent more members next year. How many members do they want to add?

They want to add _____ members.

16.

---

17. A 22-pound mixture of cashews and peanuts contains 20 percent cashews by weight. How many pounds of cashews are in the mixture?

There are _____ pounds of cashews.

17.

---

18. If 55 percent of the 1,540 students at East Side Middle School ride bikes to school, how many students ride bikes to school?

_____ students ride bikes to school.

18.

Check What You Know

Customary Measurement

Convert the following.

	a	**b**
1.	8 ft. = _____ in.	108 in. = _____ ft.
2.	720 in. = _____ yd.	3 mi. = _____ ft.
3.	11 yd. = _____ ft.	168 in. = _____ ft.
4.	7 ft. 7 in. = _____ in.	4 yd. 7 in. = _____ in.
5.	66 pt. = _____ qt.	26 qt. = _____ pt.
6.	41 qt. 1 pt. = _____ pt.	5 gal. 3 qt. = _____ qt.
7.	5 qt. 1 pt. = _____ pt.	9 qt. = _____ gal.
8.	104 qt. = _____ gal.	133 qt. = _____ pt.
9.	25 lb. = _____ oz.	60 lb. = _____ oz.
10.	23 T. = _____ lb.	8 lb. 12 oz. = _____ oz.
11.	19 lb. = _____ oz.	12 oz. = _____ lb.
12.	272 oz. = _____ lb.	58,000 lb. = _____ T.

Check What You Know

Customary Measurement

Find the perimeter of each figure.

13.

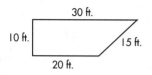
30 ft.
10 ft.
15 ft.
20 ft.

perimeter = _____ feet

12 yd. 16 yd.
8 yd.
10 yd.
24 yd.

perimeter = _____ yards

Find the area of each right triangle.

14.

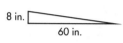
8 in.
60 in.

area = _____ square inches

25 ft.
15 ft.

area = _____ square feet

Find the volume of each rectangular solid.

15.

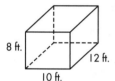
8 ft.
12 ft.
10 ft.

volume = _____ cubic feet

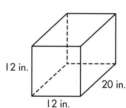
12 in.
20 in.
12 in.

volume = _____ cubic inches

SHOW YOUR WORK

Solve each problem.

16. The sail on a boat is shaped like a right triangle. Its base is 15 feet and its height is 22 feet. What is the area?

The area is _____ square feet.

16.

17. A shoe box is 6 inches wide, 10 inches long, and 5 inches high. What is the volume?

The volume is _____ cubic inches.

17.

18. A ski jump is shaped like a right triangle. It is 27 feet long and 4 feet high. What is the area of the ski jump?

The area is _____ square feet.

18.

Lesson 9.1 Units of Length (inches, feet, yards, and miles)

1 foot (ft.) = 12 inches (in.)
1 yard (yd.) = 3 ft.
1 yd. = 36 in.
1 mile (mi.) = 5,280 ft.

1 in. = $\frac{1}{12}$ ft.
1 ft. = $\frac{1}{3}$ yd.
1 in. = $\frac{1}{36}$ yd.
1 mi. = 1,760 yd.

24 in. = _____ ft.
1 in. = $\frac{1}{12}$ ft.
24 in. = (24 × $\frac{1}{12}$) ft.
24 in. = __2__ ft.

5 ft. 8 in. = _____ in.
1 ft. = 12 in.
5 ft. = (5 × 12) or 60 in.
5 ft. 8 in. = (60 + 8) in.
5 ft. 8 in. = __68__ in.

Complete the following.

	a	b	c
1.	7 ft. = _____ in.	72 in. = _____ ft.	15 yd. = _____ ft.
2.	108 in. = _____ yd.	4 mi. = _____ ft.	4 mi. = _____ yd.
3.	3 yd. = _____ ft.	120 in. = _____ ft.	42 ft. = _____ yd.
4.	4 ft. 7 in. = _____ in.	2 yd 9 in. = _____ in.	30 in. = _____ ft.
5.	15,840 ft. = _____ mi.	6 yd. = _____ ft.	6 yd. = _____ in.
6.	7 yd. 2 ft. = _____ ft.	7 yd. 2 ft. = _____ in.	24 ft. = _____ yd.
7.	11 ft. 9 in. = _____ in.	2 mi. 500 ft. = _____ ft.	52,800 ft. = _____ mi.
8.	25 ft. = _____ in.	144 in. = _____ ft.	144 in. = _____ yd.
9.	5 mi. = _____ yd.	18 in. = _____ ft.	12 yd. = _____ ft.
10.	12 yd. = _____ in.	2,640 ft. = _____ mi.	5 yd. 8 in. = _____ in.
11.	5 ft. 2 in. = _____ in.	3 mi. = _____ yd.	6 in. = _____ ft.
12.	168 in. = _____ ft.	81 ft. = _____ yd.	42 ft. = _____ yd.

Lesson 9.2 Liquid Volume (cups, pints, quarts, and gallons)

1 pint (pt.) = 2 cups (c.) $1 c. = \frac{1}{2} pt.$
1 quart (qt.) = 2 pt. $1 pt. = \frac{1}{2} qt.$
1 gallon (gal.) = 4 qt. $1 qt. = \frac{1}{4} gal.$

7 pt. = _____ qt.   2 gal. 3 qt. = _____ qt.
$1 pt. = \frac{1}{2} qt.$ 1 gal. = 4 qt.
$7 pt. = (7 \times \frac{1}{2}) qt. = \frac{7}{2} qt.$ 2 gal. = (2 × 4) or 8 qt.
$7 pt. = \underline{3\frac{1}{2}} qt.$ 2 gal. 3 qt. = (8 + 3) qt.
                                    2 gal. 3 qt. = _11_ qt.

Complete the following.

	a	b	c
1.	7 pt. = _____ c.	72 c. = _____ pt.	15 gal. = _____ qt.
2.	108 qt. = _____ gal.	4 c. = _____ pt.	4 qt. = _____ pt.
3.	3 pt. = _____ qt.	120 qt. = _____ gal.	42 pt. = _____ c.
4.	4 gal. 3 qt. = _____ qt.	9 pt. 1 c. = _____ c.	30 qt. = _____ gal.
5.	40 pt. = _____ qt.	6 qt. = _____ pt.	6 c. = _____ pt.
6.	7 qt. 1 pt. = _____ pt.	7 gal. 1 qt. = _____ qt.	24 gal. = _____ qt.
7.	11 qt. 1 pt. = _____ pt.	2 qt. = _____ gal.	52 pt. = _____ qt.
8.	52 qt. = _____ gal.	144 qt. = _____ pt.	144 qt. = _____ gal.
9.	5 gal. = _____ qt.	20 qt. = _____ pt.	5 gal. = _____ pt.
10.	10 gal. = _____ pt.	640 qt. = _____ gal.	5 pt. 1 c. = _____ c.
11.	2 qt. = _____ pt.	4 pt. = _____ c.	2 qt. = _____ c.
12.	2 qt. = _____ gal.	8 c. = _____ gal.	1 gal. = _____ c.

Lesson 9.3 Weight (ounces, pounds, and tons)

1 pound (lb.) = 16 ounces (oz.)

1 ton (T.) = 2,000 lb.

1 T. = (2,000 × 16) oz.

1 T. = 32,000 oz.

160 oz. = _____ lb.

1 oz. = $\frac{1}{16}$ lb.

160 oz. = (160 × $\frac{1}{16}$) lb.

160 oz. = __10__ lb.

1 oz. = $\frac{1}{16}$ lb.

3 T. = _____ lb.

3 T. = (3 × 32,000) lb.

3 T. = __6,000__ lb.

3 T. = _____ oz.

3 T. = (3 × 32,000) oz.

3 T. = __96,000__ oz.

Complete the following.

	a	**b**
1.	65 lb. = _____ oz.	96 oz. = _____ lb.
2.	128 oz. = _____ lb.	50 lb. = _____ oz.
3.	32 oz. = _____ lb.	4 lb. = _____ oz.
4.	5 T. = _____ lb.	7 lb. 1 oz. = _____ oz.
5.	40 lb. = _____ oz.	25,000 lb. = _____ T.
6.	12 oz. = _____ lb.	7 T. 400 lb. = _____ lb.
7.	11 lb. 8 oz. = _____ oz.	8 oz. = _____ lb.
8.	52 oz. = _____ lb.	144 oz. = _____ lb.
9.	5 lb. = _____ oz.	20 lb. = _____ oz.
10.	10 T. = _____ lb.	9 lb. 14 oz. = _____ oz.
11.	2 lb. = _____ oz.	4 oz. = _____ lb.
12.	176 oz. = _____ lb.	18,000 lb. = _____ T.

Lesson 9.4 Measuring Perimeter and Area

The **perimeter** is the distance around a figure. To find the perimeter, find the sum of the lengths of its sides.

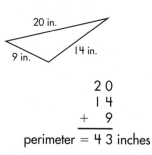

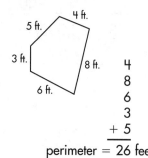

```
  2 0
  1 4
+   9
```
perimeter = 4 3 inches

```
  4
  8
  6
  3
+ 5
```
perimeter = 26 feet

The **area** (A) of a right triangle is one-half the product of the measure of its base (b) and the measure of its height (h). $A = \frac{1}{2} \times b \times h$

$A = \frac{1}{2} \times 9 \times 4$
$= \frac{1}{2} \times 36$
$= 18$
$A = 18$ square inches

$A = \frac{1}{2} \times 5 \times 7$
$= \frac{1}{2} \times 35$
$= 17\frac{1}{2}$
$A = 17\frac{1}{2}$ square feet

Find the perimeter of each figure.

     a   **b**

1.

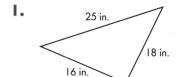

perimeter =

_____ inches

perimeter =

_____ feet

2.

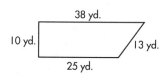

perimeter =

_____ yards

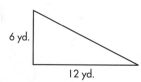

perimeter =

_____ feet

Find the area of each right triangle.

3.

area = _____

square inches

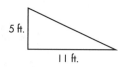

area = _____

square feet

4.

area = _____

square feet

area = _____

square yards

Lesson 9.5 Measuring Volume

The **volume** (V) measure of a rectangular solid is the product of the measure of its length (ℓ), the measure of its width (w), and the measure of its height (h). $V = ℓ \times w \times h$

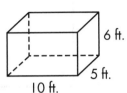

$$V = 10 \times 5 \times 6$$
$$= 50 \times 6$$
$$= 300$$

The volume is 300 cubic feet.

Find the volume of each rectangular solid.

	a	b	c

1.

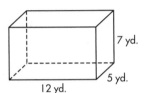 7 yd. / 5 yd. / 12 yd.

volume =

_____ cubic yards

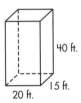 8 in. / 8 in. / 8 in.

volume =

_____ cubic inches

  40 ft. / 15 ft. / 20 ft.

volume =

_____ cubic feet

2.

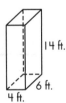 14 ft. / 6 ft. / 4 ft.

volume =

_____ cubic feet

  5 in. / 5 in. / 4 in.

volume =

_____ cubic inches

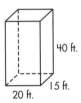 9 in. / 12 in. / 6 in.

volume =

_____ cubic inches

3.

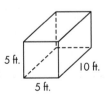 5 ft. / 10 ft. / 5 ft.

volume =

_____ cubic feet

  5 in. / 15 in. / 4 in.

volume =

_____ cubic inches

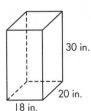 30 in. / 20 in. / 18 in.

volume =

_____ cubic inches

Lesson 9.6 Problem Solving

SHOW YOUR WORK

Solve each problem.

1. Mr. Ruiz wants to put a fence around his backyard. The yard is a rectangle 50 feet long and 28 feet wide. How many feet of fence will he need?

   Mr. Ruiz will need _____ feet of fence.

2. Andrew has an aquarium that is 16 inches long, 10 inches wide, and 9 inches deep. What is the volume of Andrew's aquarium?

   The volume of Andrew's aquarium is _____ cubic inches.

3. A city park is shaped like a right triangle. Its base is 20 yards and its depth is 48 yards. What is the area of the park?

   The area of the park is _____ square yards.

   The third side of the park is 52 yards. What is the perimeter of the park?

   The perimeter is _____ yards.

4. A paving brick is 3 inches wide, 2 inches high, and 6 inches long. What is the volume of the brick?

   The volume is _____ cubic inches.

5. A tabletop is shaped like a right triangle with a base of 25 inches and a depth of 30 inches. What is the area of the tabletop?

   The area of the tabletop is _____ square inches.

6. A baseball diamond has 3 bases and home plate that are each 90 feet apart. How many feet will a batter run if he hits a home run?

   The batter will run _____ feet.

1.

2.

3.

4.

5.

6.

Check What You Learned

Customary Measurement

Convert the following.

a   b

1. 9 ft. = _____ in.   84 in. = _____ ft.

2. 180 in. = _____ yd.   6 mi. = _____ ft.

3. 9 yd. = _____ ft.   180 in. = _____ ft.

4. 6 ft. 7 in. = _____ in.   10 yd. 9 in. = _____ in.

5. 50 pt. = _____ qt.   16 qt. = _____ pt.

6. 21 qt. 1 pt. = _____ pt.   3 gal. 1 qt. = _____ qt.

7. 1 qt. 1 pt. = _____ pt.   6 qt. = _____ gal.

8. 92 qt. = _____ gal.   172 qt. = _____ pt.

9. 15 lb. = _____ oz.   30 lb. = _____ oz.

10. 20 T. = _____ lb.   6 lb. 12 oz. = _____ oz.

11. 12 lb. = _____ oz.   8 oz. = _____ lb.

12. 208 oz. = _____ lb.   28,000 lb. = _____ T.

Check What You Learned

Customary Measurement

CHAPTER 9 POSTTEST

Find the perimeter of each figure.

13. 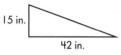 32 in. 20 in. 12 in. 25 in.

perimeter = _____ inches

12 ft. 55 ft. 15 ft. 15 ft. 42 ft.

perimeter = _____ feet

Find the area of each right triangle.

14. 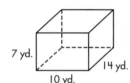 15 in. 42 in.

area = _____ square inches

17 ft. 9 ft.

area = _____ square feet

Find the volume of each rectangular solid.

15. 7 yd. 10 yd. 14 yd.

volume = _____ cubic yards

20 ft. 20 ft. 28 ft.

volume = _____ cubic feet

SHOW YOUR WORK

Solve each problem.

16. A piece of metal is shaped like a right triangle. Its base is 18 feet and its height is 24 feet. What is its area?

The area is _____ square feet.

16.

17. Stefanie's hamster cage is 20 inches long, 12 inches wide, and 10 inches deep. What is the volume of the cage?

The volume is _____ cubic inches.

17.

18. Pablo's snake cage is 28 inches long, 15 inches wide, and 12 inches deep. What is the volume of the cage?

The volume is _____ cubic inches.
How many cubic feet is the volume of the cage?

The cage is _____ cubic feet.

18.

Check What You Know

Metric Measurement

Complete the following.

	a	b	c
1.	58 cm = _____ mm	58 mm = _____ cm	58 cm = _____ m
2.	2.6 km = _____ m	6.2 m = _____ km	50 mm = _____ m
3.	725 cm = _____ m	638 cm = _____ mm	0.46 m = _____ mm
4.	5 L = _____ mL	7 L = _____ kL	350 mL = _____ L
5.	5 mL = _____ L	0.6 kL = _____ L	0.081 L = _____ mL
6.	3.8 mL = _____ L	5.4 L = _____ kL	1.4 L = _____ mL
7.	9,500 g = _____ kg	40 g = _____ kg	7 g = _____ kg
8.	4 kg = _____ g	0.38 kg = _____ g	53 mg = _____ g
9.	0.42 g = _____ mg	57 mg = _____ g	6.2 g = _____ mg

NAME _____

Check What You Know

Metric Measurement

Find the perimeter of each figure.

a	b	c

10.

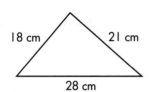

18 cm 21 cm
28 cm

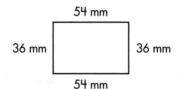

54 mm
36 mm 36 mm
54 mm

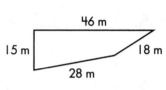

46 m
15 m 18 m
28 m

perimeter = _____ cm   perimeter = _____ mm   perimeter = _____ m

Find the area of each rectangle.

11.

6.8 cm
10.2 cm

32 m
32 m

108 mm
62 mm

area = _____ sq. cm   area = _____ sq. m   area = _____ sq. mm

Find the volume of each rectangular solid.

12.

8 cm 15 cm
10 cm

15 mm
15 mm 12 mm

4 m 8 m
12 m

volume = _____ cu. cm   volume = _____ cu. mm   volume = _____ cu. m

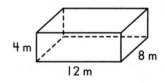

SHOW YOUR WORK

Solve each problem.

13. A jar contains 3.5 liters of liquid that will be divided evenly into bottles which can each hold 70 milliliters of liquid. How many bottles can be filled?

_____ bottles can be filled.

13.

14. A nickel weighs about 5 grams. There are 40 coins in a roll of nickels. How much do 12 rolls of nickels weigh?

The rolls of nickels weigh _____ kilograms.

14.

Lesson 10.1 Units of Length (millimeters, centimeters, meters, and kilometers)

Metric units of length are **millimeters** (mm), **centimeters** (cm), **meters** (m), and **kilometers** (km).

380 m = _____ km
  1 m = 0.001 km
380 m = (380 × 0.001) km
380 m = 0.38 km

10 mm = 1 cm
1,000 mm = 1 m
100 cm = 1 m
1,000 m = 1 km

1 mm = 0.1 cm
1 mm = 0.001 m
1 cm = 0.01 m
1 m = 0.001 km

9.3 cm = _____ cm
  1 cm = 10 mm
7.2 cm = (7.2 × 10) mm
7.2 cm = 72 mm

Complete the following.

	a	b	c
1.	46 mm = _____ cm	46 mm = _____ m	350 m = _____ km
2.	2.3 m = _____ cm	3.2 m = _____ mm	3.2 m = _____ km
3.	5.2 mm = _____ cm	7.6 mm = _____ m	6.7 cm = _____ mm
4.	3 km = _____ m	42 mm = _____ cm	42 m = _____ km
5.	0.06 m = _____ cm	38.5 m = _____ km	38.5 m = _____ cm
6.	13 mm = _____ m	0.08 cm = _____ mm	0.8 cm = _____ m
7.	342 m = _____ km	0.4 m = _____ cm	500 m = _____ km
8.	645 mm = _____ cm	58 cm = _____ mm	8,730 m = _____ km
9.	583 cm = _____ mm	32 km = _____ m	5 km = _____ m
10.	0.3 cm = _____ mm	3 cm = _____ mm	45 m = _____ mm

Lesson 10.4 Measuring Perimeter and Area

The **perimeter** is the sum of the lengths of the sides.

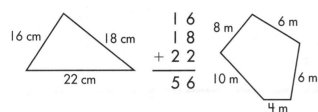

```
  1 6
  1 8
+ 2 2
_____
  5 6
```

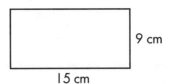

perimeter = 56 cm   perimeter = 34 m

To find the **area** (A) of a rectangle, multiply the measure of its length (ℓ) by the measure of its width (w).

9 cm

15 cm

area = ℓ × w = 15 × 9 = 135 square cm

Find the perimeter of each figure.

1.

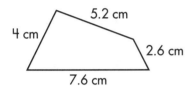

4 cm · 5.2 cm · 2.6 cm · 7.6 cm

perimeter = _____ cm

2.

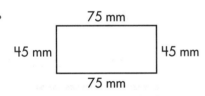

75 mm · 45 mm · 45 mm · 75 mm

perimeter = _____ mm

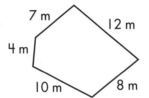

7 m · 12 m · 4 m · 10 m · 8 m

perimeter = _____ m

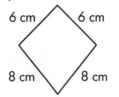

6 cm · 6 cm · 8 cm · 8 cm

perimeter = _____ cm

Find the area.

3.

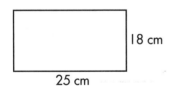

18 cm

25 cm

area = _____ square cm

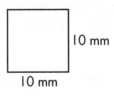

10 mm

10 mm

area = _____ square mm

4.

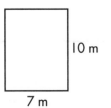

10 m

7 m

area = _____ square m

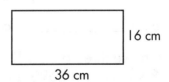

16 cm

36 cm

area = _____ square cm

Lesson 10.1 Units of Length (millimeters, centimeters, meters, and kilometers)

Metric units of length are **millimeters** (mm), **centimeters** (cm), **meters** (m), and **kilometers** (km).

380 m = _____ km
  1 m = 0.001 km
380 m = (380 × 0.001) km
380 m = 0.38 km

9.3 cm = _____ cm
  1 cm = 10 mm
7.2 cm = (7.2 × 10) mm
7.2 cm = 72 mm

10 mm = 1 cm	1 mm = 0.1 cm
1,000 mm = 1 m	1 mm = 0.001 m
100 cm = 1 m	1 cm = 0.01 m
1,000 m = 1 km	1 m = 0.001 km

Complete the following.

	a	b	c
1.	46 mm = _____ cm	46 mm = _____ m	350 m = _____ km
2.	2.3 m = _____ cm	3.2 m = _____ mm	3.2 m = _____ km
3.	5.2 mm = _____ cm	7.6 mm = _____ m	6.7 cm = _____ mm
4.	3 km = _____ m	42 mm = _____ cm	42 m = _____ km
5.	0.06 m = _____ cm	38.5 m = _____ km	38.5 m = _____ cm
6.	13 mm = _____ m	0.08 cm = _____ mm	0.8 cm = _____ m
7.	342 m = _____ km	0.4 m = _____ cm	500 m = _____ km
8.	645 mm = _____ cm	58 cm = _____ mm	8,730 m = _____ km
9.	583 cm = _____ mm	32 km = _____ m	5 km = _____ m
10.	0.3 cm = _____ mm	3 cm = _____ mm	45 m = _____ mm

Lesson 10.2 Liquid Volume (milliliters, liters, and kiloliters)

Metric units of liquid volume are **milliliters** (mL), **liters** (L), and **kiloliters** (kL).

73 L = _____ mL   35 L = _____ kL

1 L = 1000 mL   1 L = 0.001 kL

73 L = (73 × 1000) mL   35 L = (35 × 0.001) kL

73 L = 73,000 mL   35 L = 0.035 kL

1 L	= 1000 cm
1000 L	= 1 kL
1 mL	= 0.001 L
1 L	= 0.001 kL

Complete the following.

	a	b	c
1.	2 L = _____ mL	2 L = _____ kL	2 kL = _____ L
2.	33 mL = _____ L	4.22 kL = _____ L	40 mL = _____ L
3.	2.73 kL = _____ L	273 mL = _____ L	40 L = _____ mL
4.	800 mL = _____ L	450 L = _____ kL	12 mL = _____ L
5.	5.2 mL = _____ L	5.2 L = _____ kL	3,760 mL = _____ L
6.	7,600 L = _____ kL	3,500 mL = _____ L	5 L = _____ mL

SHOW YOUR WORK

Solve each problem.

7. A container holds 800 milliliters of liquid that will be divided evenly among 16 bottles. How much liquid will go into each bottle.

_____ milliliters of liquid will go into each bottle.

7.

8. How many 500-milliliter bottles can be filled from a 300-liter container of liquid?

_____ bottles can be filled.

8.

9. An orange juice container is marked 1.89 liters. How many milliliters of orange juice are there?

There are _____ milliliters of orange juice.

9.

Lesson 10.3 Weight (milligrams, grams, and kilograms)

Metric units of weight are **milligrams** (mg), **grams** (g), and **kilograms** (kg).

63 kg = _____ g	32 mg = _____ g	
1 kg = 1000 g	1 mg = 0.001 g	
63 kg = (63 × 1000) g	32 mg = (32 × 0.001) g	
63 kg = 63,000 g	32 mg = 0.032 g	

1 g = 1000 mg
1 kg = 1000 g
1 mg = 0.001 g
1 g = 0.001 kg

Complete the following.

	a	b	c
1.	4 kg = _____ g	4 g = _____ kg	4 g = _____ mg
2.	73 mg = _____ g	3.66 kg = _____ g	30 mg = _____ g
3.	2.6 kg = _____ g	265 g = _____ kg	40 g = _____ mg
4.	900 g = _____ kg	0.72 g = _____ mg	0.8 g = _____ kg
5.	492 g = _____ kg	6 g = _____ kg	6 g = _____ mg
6.	86,400 g = _____ kg	1.2 kg = _____ g	4 mg = _____ g

SHOW YOUR WORK

Solve each problem.

7. A nickel weighs about 5 grams. A roll of nickels contains 40 coins. How much do 8 rolls of nickels weigh?

   The nickels weigh about _____ kilograms.

7.

8. A truck is carrying 8 crates, each weighing 55 kilograms. What is the total weight of the crates?

   The crates weigh _____ kilograms.

8.

9. Tara needs to move three boxes. The weights of the boxes are 3.8 kilograms, 4,590 grams, and 3 kilograms. What is the total weight of the boxes?

   The boxes weigh _____ kilograms.

9.

Lesson 10.4 Measuring Perimeter and Area

The **perimeter** is the sum of the lengths of the sides.

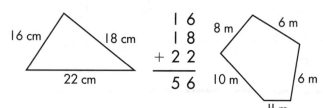

perimeter = 56 cm   perimeter = 34 m

To find the **area** (A) of a rectangle, multiply the measure of its length (ℓ) by the measure of its width (w).

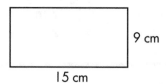

area = ℓ × w = 15 × 9 = 135 square cm

Find the perimeter of each figure.

1.

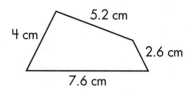

perimeter = _____ cm

2.

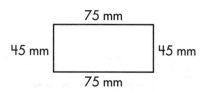

perimeter = _____ mm

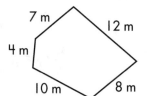

perimeter = _____ m

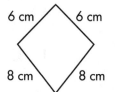

perimeter = _____ cm

Find the area.

3.

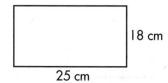

area = _____ square cm

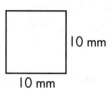

area = _____ square mm

4.

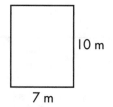

area = _____ square m

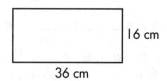

area = _____ square cm

Lesson 10.5 Measuring Volume

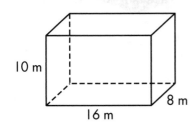

Volume = length (ℓ) × width (w) × height (h)
Volume = (16 × 8 × 10) cubic m
Volume = 1,280 cubic m

Find the volume of each rectangular solid.

	a	b	c

1.

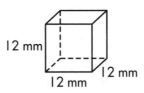

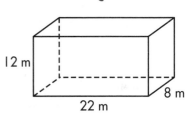

volume = _____ cu. cm   volume = _____ cu. mm   volume = _____ cu. m

2.

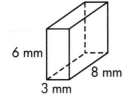

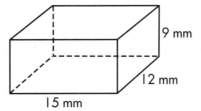

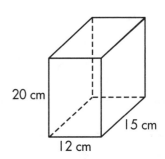

volume = _____ cu. mm   volume = _____ cu. mm   volume = _____ cu. cm

3.

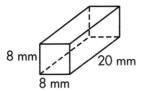

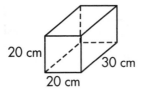

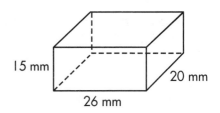

volume = _____ cu. mm   volume = _____ cu. mm   volume = _____ cu. mm

Lesson 10.6 Problem Solving

Solve each problem.

1. Craig's backyard is a rectangle 25 meters long and 20 meters wide. What is the perimeter of Craig's yard?

   The perimeter of Craig's yard is _____ meters.

   1.

2. A shipping crate is 0.85 meter long, 0.4 meter wide, and 0.3 meter high. What is the volume of the crate?

   The crate's volume is _____ cubic meter.

   2.

3. A rectangular poster is 45 centimeters long and 28 centimeters wide. What is the area of the poster?

   The poster's area is _____ square centimeters.

   3.

4. A room is 8.6 meters wide and 10.2 meters long. What is the area of the room?

   The area of the room is _____ square meters.

   4.

5. Megan's jewelry box is 25 centimeters long, 12 centimeters wide, and 10 centimeters high. What is the volume of Megan's jewelry box?

   The volume of Megan's jewelry box is _____ cubic centimeters.

   5.

6. A rectangular CD jewel case is approximately 14 centimeters long and 12 centimeters wide. What is the perimeter of the CD jewel case?

   The perimeter of the jewel case is _____ centimeters.

   6.

Lesson 10.7 Equivalent Measurements

Liquid Volume	
To convert	Multiply by
quart (qt.) to liter (L)	0.946
gallon (gal.) to liter	3.785
pint (pt.) to liter	0.473
cup (c.) to liter	0.237
ounce (oz.) to milliliter (mL)	29.574

Weight	
To convert	Multiply by
ounce (oz.) to gram (g)	28.35
pound (lb.) to kilogram (kg)	0.454
ounce to milligram (mg)	28,350
ounce to kilogram (kg)	0.028

Length	
To convert	Multiply by
inch (in.) to millimeter (mm)	25.4
inch to centimeter (cm)	2.54
feet (ft.) to meter (m)	0.305
yard (yd.) to meter	0.914
mile (mi.) to kilometer (km)	1.609

3 qt. = _____ L

$3 \times 0.0946 = 2.838$

Round to the nearest hundredth.

3 qt. = 2.84 L

5 lb. = _____ kg

$5 \times 0.454 = 2.27$

5 lb. = 2.27 kg

3 mi. = _____ km

$3 \times 1.609 = 4.827$

Round to the nearest hundredth.

3 mi. = 4.83 km

Complete the following. Round your answers to the nearest hundredth.

	a	b	c
1.	10 lb. = _____ kg	35 oz. = _____ mg	5 oz. = _____ g
2.	20 oz. = _____ kg	17 lb. = _____ kg	45 oz. = _____ kg
3.	350 oz. = _____ mg	7 oz. = _____ kg	100 lb. = _____ kg
4.	2,500 oz. = _____ kg	100 oz. = _____ g	7 oz. = _____ mg
5.	10 in. = _____ mm	72 ft. = _____ m	31 mi. = _____ km
6.	37 in. = _____ cm	43 yd. = _____ m	132 ft. = _____ m

Lesson 10.7 Equivalent Measurements (metric and customary)

Complete the following. Round your answers to the nearest hundredth.

	a	**b**	**c**
1.	9 mi. = _____ km	55 in. = _____ cm	82 in. = _____ mm
2.	100 ft. = _____ m	21 yd. = _____ m	1,000 in. = _____ mm
3.	10 c. = _____ L	12 qt. = _____ L	7 gal. = _____ L
4.	70 pt. = _____ L	700 gal. = _____ L	2 qt. = _____ L
5.	10 oz. = _____ mL	35 c. = _____ L	22 pt. = _____ L
6.	97 gal. = _____ L	54 oz. = _____ mL	38 pt. = _____ L

Compare each measurement using $<$, $>$, or $=$.

7. 2 in. _____ 5 cm	1 ft. _____ 60 cm	1 yd. _____ 2.7 m
8. 56 oz. _____ 75 g	4 qt. _____ 5 L	10 gal. _____ 38 L
9. 8 c. _____ 2 L	15 lb. _____ 5 kg	12 mi. _____ 12 km
10. 22 oz. _____ 20 mL	10 oz. _____ 280 g	15 yd. _____ 13.5 m

Check What You Learned

Metric Measurement

Complete the following.

	a	b	c
1.	65 cm = _____ mm	65 mm = _____ cm	65 cm = _____ m
2.	5.8 km = _____ m	7.2 m = _____ km	70 mm = _____ m
3.	867 cm = _____ m	368 cm = _____ mm	0.92 m = _____ mm
4.	8 L = _____ mL	3 L = _____ kL	530 mL = _____ L
5.	8 mL = _____ L	0.9 kL = _____ L	0.034 L = _____ mL
6.	2.2 mL = _____ L	3.7 L = _____ kL	6.1 L = _____ mL
7.	8,700 g = _____ kg	80 g = _____ kg	5 g = _____ kg
8.	2 kg = _____ g	0.27 kg = _____ g	77 mg = _____ g
9.	0.38 g = _____ mg	63 mg = _____ g	5.7 g = _____ mg

Check What You Learned

Metric Measurement

Find the perimeter of each figure.

a	b	c

10.

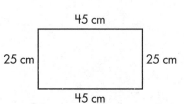

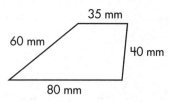

$P =$ _____ m

$P =$ _____ cm

$P =$ _____ mm

Find the area of each rectangle.

11.

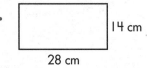

$A =$ _____ square cm

$A =$ _____ square m

$A =$ _____ square mm

Find the volume of each rectangular solid.

12.

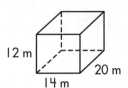

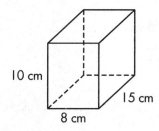

$V =$ _____ cubic m

$V =$ _____ cubic mm

$V =$ _____ cubic cm

SHOW YOUR WORK

Solve each problem.

13. A container that holds 2.4 liters of liquid will be divided evenly into bottles which each hold 80 milliliters of liquid. How many bottles can be filled?

_____ bottles can be filled.

13.

14. A pencil eraser weighs about 5 grams. There are 40 erasers in a pack. How much do 16 packs weigh?

The packs weigh _____ kilograms.

14.

Check What You Know

Probability and Statistics

Use the line graph to answer each question.

Angelica and Lucy are on a fitness program. They are keeping track of how far they walk. They record their totals after each week.

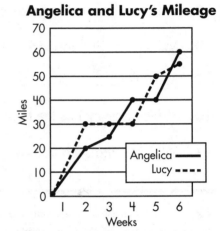

Angelica and Lucy's Mileage

1. After two weeks, how much farther did Lucy walk than Angelica? _____

2. During what week did Angelica not walk? _____

3. Who walked farthest during the 6 weeks? _____

4. How much farther did she walk? _____

Complete.

5. Draw a stem and leaf plot for the following set of numbers.
   25, 18, 36, 24, 31, 56, and 72

6. Find mean, median, mode, and range of the following set of numbers.
   97, 82, 66, 98, 66, 85, 82, 66, and 78

   mean _____   mode _____

   median _____   range _____

7. A bag contains 3 red marbles, 5 blue marbles, and 7 white marbles. One marble is pulled out at random. Find the probability of the following.

   P (red) _____   P (not white) _____

   P (blue) _____   P (blue or white) _____

NAME _____

Check What You Know

Probability and Statistics

Use the circle graph to answer these questions.

After School Activities

8. What is the most popular after-school activity? _____

9. Which activity appears to be half as popular as

    sports? _____

10. Which activity has the least amount of participation? _____

11. Which is the second most popular activity? _____

12. The spinner shown will be spun twice. Draw a tree diagram to show the outcomes. How many outcomes will have the same color come up twice?

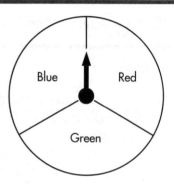

13. Find the mean, median, mode, and range of the following set of numbers.
    8, 14, 6, 12, 12, 12, 20

    mean _____   mode _____

    median _____   range _____

14. The spinner shown is spun. Find the probabilities.

    P (2) _____ P (even) _____

    P (odd) _____ P (not 3) _____

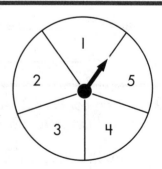

Lesson 11.1 Reading Bar Graphs

The bar graph shows the after-school activities of males and females in Mrs. Martin's class.

How many females participate in the Student Council? __5__

How many males participate in the Student Council? __3__

How many more females than males participate in the Student Council? __2__

After-School Activities in Mrs. Martin's Class

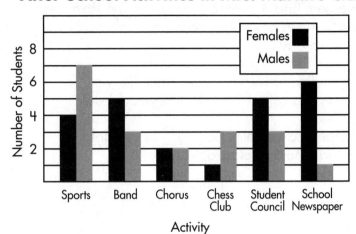

Use the bar graph above to answer the following questions.

1. Which activity has the same number of females as males? _____

2. What is the most popular activity for males? _____

3. What is the most popular activity for females? _____

4. How many more females than males are in the band? _____

5. How many females are in either band or chorus? _____

6. How many more males than females participate in sports? _____

7. How many males participate in either band or sports? _____

8. Which activity has the least number of males? _____

9. What is the total number of participants in sports? _____

10. Which activity has the greatest difference between females and males? _____

Lesson 11.2 Reading Line Graphs

Mrs. Martin's homeroom and Mr. Lopez's homeroom had a canned food drive. The **line graph** shows how many cans were collected after each day.

On Monday, how many more cans did Mr. Lopez's class collect than Mrs. Martin's class?

Mr. Lopez's class collected ___5___ more cans than Mrs. Martin's class on Monday.

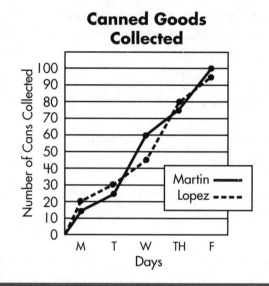

Canned Goods Collected

Use the line graph above to answer the following questions.

1. On Monday, whose homeroom collected the most cans? _____

2. On Tuesday, how many cans did Mr. Lopez's homeroom collect? _____

3. On which day was the difference between the number of cans collected by each homeroom the greatest? _____

4. Which homeroom collected the most cans on that day? _____

5. How many cans were collected by both homerooms on Tuesday? _____

6. On what day did Mrs. Martin's homeroom bring in the most cans? _____

7. On what day did Mr. Lopez's homeroom bring in the most cans? _____

8. On what day did Mrs. Martin's homeroom bring in the least number of cans? _____

9. On Wednesday, how many cans were collected by both homerooms? _____

10. How many cans were collected by both homerooms during the week? _____

Lesson 11.3 Reading Circle Graphs

A **circle graph** is used to show the relationship of the parts of a group to the whole group. The circle represents the whole group and the sections represent the parts. The circle graph at the right shows the different-colored cats at a cat shelter. On a given day at the shelter there are 16 cats. Eight are gray, 4 are black, 2 are calico, and 2 are tabby.

Colors of Cats at the Animal Shelter

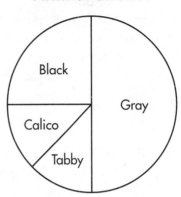

The Floral Shop received 40 orders in one day. The distribution is shown in the circle graph.

1. Which were the most popular flowers? _____

2. How many orders were for roses? _____

3. How many orders were for mums? _____

4. How many orders were for carnations? _____

5. How many orders were for daisies? _____

Orders at The Floral Shop

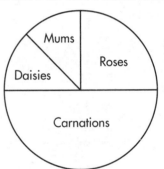

An order of roses costs $30, an order of daisies costs $18, an order of mums costs $15, and an order of carnations costs $15.

6. How much money was made from selling roses? _____

7. How much money was made from selling daisies? _____

8. How much money was made from selling mums? _____

9. How much money was made from selling carnations? _____

10. What was the total amount of money made from selling all of the flowers in

    one day? _____

Lesson 11.4 Measures of Central Tendency

The **mean** is the average of a set of numbers. To find the mean, add all the numbers and divide by the number of addends.

The **median** is the middle number of a set of numbers. If there are two middle numbers, the median is the average of the two.

The **mode** is the number that appears most often in a set of numbers.

The **range** is the difference between the greatest and the least number of the set.

Example: 12, 15, 18, 23, 8, 10, and 12

Mean: $12 + 15 + 18 + 23 + 8 + 10 + 12 = 98$ $\frac{98}{7} = 14$

To find the median, arrange the numbers in order.   8, 10, 12, <u>12</u>, 15, 18, 23

Median: 12   Mode: 12   Range: $23 - 8 = 15$

Find the median of 8, 6, 5, 7, 2, and 10.   2, 5, <u>6</u>, <u>7</u>, 8, 10

The middle numbers are 6 and 7.   Median is $\frac{13}{2} = 6\frac{1}{2}$.

Find the mean, median, mode, and range of each set of numbers. Show your work.

	a	**b**

1. 32, 35, 25, 43, 43   8, 12, 23, 12, 15

mean _____   mean _____

median _____   median _____

mode _____   mode _____

range _____   range _____

2. 10, 18, 12, 14, 12, 12   17, 15, 15, 28, 20, 26

mean _____   mean _____

median _____   median _____

mode _____   mode _____

range _____   range _____

3. 52, 61, 79, 78, 56, 79, 71   37, 50, 67, 83, 34, 49, 37

mean _____   mean _____

median _____   median _____

mode _____   mode _____

range _____   range _____

Lesson 11.5 Stem-and-Leaf Plots

A set of data can be organized into a **stem-and-leaf plot** by using place values.

87, 38, 35, 76, 48, 57, 68, 44, 63, 49, 63, 64, 71

The tens digits are the stems and the ones digits are the leaves.

Stem	Leaves
3	5 8
4	4 8 9
5	7
6	3 3 4 8
7	1 6
8	7

This allows you to see the least (35), the largest (87), the range (52), the median (63), and the mode (63).

Key: 3 | 5 = 35

Create a stem-and-leaf plot for each set of data below. Include a key for each plot. Show your work.

	a	b
1.	14, 31, 34, 21, 13, 28, 33	63, 38, 72, 54, 50, 79, 64, 39, 57, 49
2.	48, 38, 34, 25, 27, 37, 49	88, 96, 99, 75, 87, 93, 81, 84, 91, 73
3.	19, 25, 38, 17, 24, 33, 13	26, 37, 25, 33, 35, 46, 27, 45, 23, 41

Lesson 11.6 Box-and-Whisker Plots

Box-and-whisker plots are helpful in interpreting the distribution of data.
For example, the results of a test might include these 15 scores:

   66, 56, 75, 77, 98, 72, 48, 83, 73, 89, 65, 74, 87, 85, 81

The numbers should be arranged in order:

   48, 56, 65, 66, 72, 73, 74, 75, 77, 81, 83, 85, 87, 89, 98

The median is 75. The **lower quartile** is the median of the lower half (66). The **upper quartile** is the median of the upper half (85). Draw a box around the median with its ends going through the quartiles. Each quartile contains one-fourth of the scores.

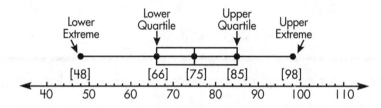

Answer the questions using the box-and-whisker plot above.

1. Half of the students scored higher than _____ on the test.

2. _____ scores are represented in the box part of the plot.

3. The range of the scores on the test is _____.

The scores on a recent daily quiz were 10, 15, 20, 20, 30, 30, 40.

4. What is the median of these scores? _____

5. What is the lower quartile? _____

6. What is the upper quartile? _____

7. Using the number line below, draw a box-and-whisker plot for these scores.

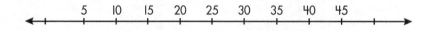

Lesson 11.7 Making Tree Diagrams

At a deli, ham or turkey sandwiches are available. Each sandwich can be made with white, rye, or wheat bread. A **tree diagram** is useful to find the number of possible combinations.

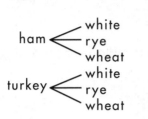

ham on white bread
ham on rye bread
ham on wheat bread
turkey on white bread
turkey on rye bread
turkey on wheat bread

There are 6 possible outcomes.

Make a tree diagram for each situation.

1. At camp, Maria has two pair of shorts—one black and one brown—and two shirts—one white and one yellow. She also has a pair of sneakers and a pair of sandals. Draw a tree diagram to show how many wardrobe combinations she has.

2. Jerry will toss a coin twice. Draw a tree diagram to show how many outcomes the two coin tosses will have.

3. Marcus will spin the spinner shown below twice. Draw a tree diagram to show how many outcomes the two spins will have. How many of those outcomes will result in

   two odd numbers? _____

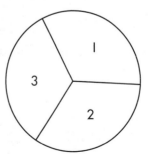

Lesson 11.8 Calculating Probability

The **probability** of an event is the measure of how likely it is that the event will occur.

$$\text{Probability } (P) = \frac{\text{number of favorable outcomes}}{\text{number of possible outcomes}}$$

A bag contains 12 marbles, 7 blue and 5 red. If a marble is chosen at random, the probability that it will be red is:

$$\text{Probability } (P) = \frac{5}{12} \quad \begin{array}{l} \text{— the number of red marbles} \\ \text{— the total number of marbles} \end{array}$$

Solve each problem.

1. A bag contains 5 blue marbles, 3 red marbles, and 2 white marbles. What is the probability a selected marble will be red? _____

   What is the probability that a selected marble will not be white? _____

   What is the probability that a selected marble will be either blue or white? _____

Use the spinner to find the following probabilities.

2. $P(3) =$ _____

3. $P(\text{odd}) =$ _____

4. $P(1 \text{ or } 4) =$ _____

5. $P(> 4) =$ _____

6. $P(< 6) =$ _____

7. $P(\text{not } 5 \text{ or } 3) =$ _____

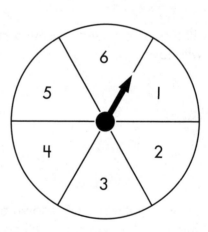

Check What You Learned

Probability and Statistics

Use the line graph to answer each question.

Lucas and Patrick are working to save money for basketball camp. They compared their savings for 6 months.

1. After 1 month, how much more money did Patrick have

   than Lucas? _____

2. During what month did Lucas save the most?

   _____

3. Who saved the most during the 6 months? _____

4. How much did they both save altogether? _____

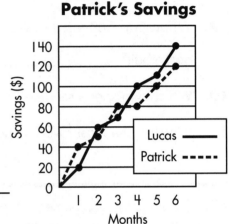

Lucas and Patrick's Savings

5. Draw a stem-and-leaf plot for the following set of numbers.
   38, 25, 22, 18, 12, 36, 31, 22

6. Find mean, median, mode, and range of the following set of numbers.
   45, 38, 52, 47, 33, 54, 47, 39, 41

   mean _____   mode _____

   median _____   range _____

7. A box of paint cans contains 5 black cans, 3 yellow cans, and 4 green cans. One can is pulled out at random. Find the probability of the following.

   P (black) _____   P (not green) _____

   P (yellow) _____   P (green or yellow) _____

Check What You Learned

Probability and Statistics

Use the circle graph to answer these questions.

8. What is the most popular sport? _____

9. What sport appears to be about half as popular as basketball? _____

10. Which two sports seem to be equal? _____

11. Which is the least favorite sport? _____

Favorite Sports

12. A coin is tossed 3 times. Draw a tree diagram showing the outcomes. How many outcomes will have the coin landing the same on all three tosses?

13. Find the mean, median, mode, and range of the following set of numbers.
9, 15, 7, 13, 13, 13, 21

mean _____   mode _____

median _____   range _____

14. Use the spinner to answer the questions.

P (3) _____   P (> 5) _____

P (odd) _____   P (< 5) _____

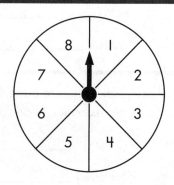

NAME _____

Check What You Know

Geometry

Match each figure with its description.

1.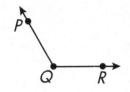
   A •———• B   _____

2.
   C •←———• D   _____

3.
   E •←———→• F   _____

A. line *AB*	E. line *CD*	J. line *EF*
B. segment *AB*	F. ray *CD*	K. ray *EF*
C. ray *AB*	G. ray *DC*	L. ray *FE*
D. ray *BA*	H. segment *CD*	M. segment *EF*

Name the angles and tell if they are acute (A), obtuse (O), or right (R). Measure them.

4.

  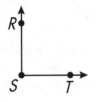

_____   _____   _____

_____   _____   _____

_____   _____   _____

Identify each pair of angles as vertical (V), supplementary (S), or complementary (C).

5. ∠A and ∠C _____

6. ∠A and ∠B _____

7. ∠B and ∠D _____

8. ∠B and ∠C _____

9. ∠X and ∠Y _____

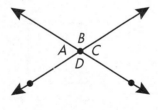 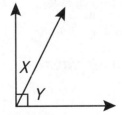

10. Identify the triangles as acute (A), obtuse (O), or right (R).

          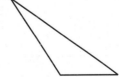   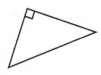

_____   _____   _____   _____

Spectrum Math
Grade 6

Check What You Know
Chapter 12
139

NAME _____

Check What You Know

Geometry

Use the circle to answer the questions.

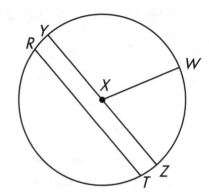

11. Name the circle. _____

12. Name the origin of the circle. _____

13. Name a radius. _____

14. Name a chord. _____

15. Name a diameter. _____

Complete.

16. Write if the following pairs of polygons are congruent (C) or not (N).

_____   _____

Match each term with its picture. You may use a letter more than once. A question may have more than one answer.

17. trapezoid   _____

18. triangular pyramid   _____

19. rhombus   _____

20. cone   _____

21. kite   _____

22. cylinder   _____

23. square   _____

24. cube   _____

25. rectangle   _____

26. triangular solid   _____

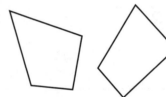

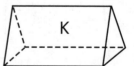

Check What You Know
Chapter 12

Lesson 12.1 Points, Lines, and Rays

A **point** has no dimensions but defines a location in space.

Points are usually named by the capital letter. $A \bullet$

A **line** extends infinitely in both directions.

A **line** is named by choosing any two points on a line.

Line BC ($\overleftrightarrow{BC}$) is the same as line CB ($\overleftrightarrow{CB}$).

A **line segment** is part of a line that begins at one point and ends at another.

Segment DE ($\overline{DE}$) is the same as segment ED ($\overline{ED}$).

A **ray** is an infinitely long part of a line that begins at a point called a vertex.
To name a ray, choose another point on the ray and name it from its vertex.

This is ray FG ($\overrightarrow{FG}$). It is not ray GF because G is not its vertex.

Draw and name the following figures. Number 1 is given.

	a			**b**	
1. line AB		$\overline{AB}$	line segment CD		$\overline{CD}$
2. ray FG	F G	____	ray GF	F G	____
3. line segment HK	H K	____	line HK	H K	____
4. line segment KH	H K	____	ray HK	H K	____
5. line CD	C D	____	line segment DC	C D	____

Identify and name.

	a			**b**	
6. P Q	____	____	P Q	____	____
7. R S	____	____	R S	____	____
8. T	____	____	M N	____	____
9. K L	____	____	K L	____	____
10. A B	____	____	A B	____	____

Lesson 12.2 Measuring Angles

An **angle** (∠) is formed by two rays which have a common vertex.

The angle is named ABC (∠ABC) or CBA (∠CBA). The **vertex**, the point where two rays meet, is always in the middle of the angle name. The measure of ∠ABC is 45°.

If the measure of an angle is less than 90°, it is an acute angle.	If the measure of an angle is 90°, it is a right angle.	If the measure of an angle is more than 90°, it is an obtuse angle.
This angle (∠) is formed by $\vec{BA}$ and $\vec{BC}$.	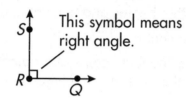 This symbol means right angle. ∠QRS is a right angle.	∠CDF is obtuse. 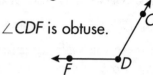 The measure of ∠CDF is 117°.

Name each angle. Write whether it is acute (A), right (R), or obtuse (O). Then, measure the angle.

1.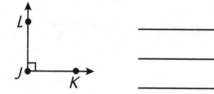

_____

_____

_____

5.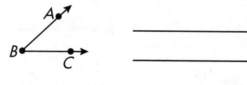

_____

_____

_____

2.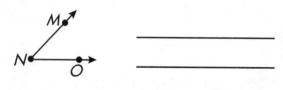

_____

_____

_____

6.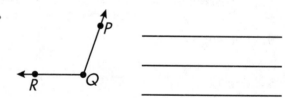

_____

_____

_____

3.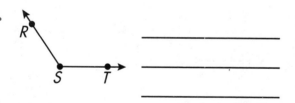

_____

_____

_____

7.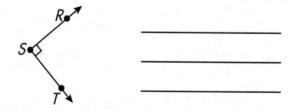

_____

_____

_____

4.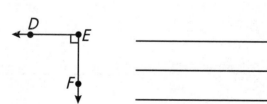

_____

_____

_____

8.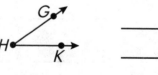

_____

_____

_____

Lesson 12.3 Types of Angles

Vertical angles are formed when two straight lines intersect. They are opposite angles and are equal in measure. ∠A and ∠C are a pair of vertical angles. ∠B and ∠D are also vertical angles.

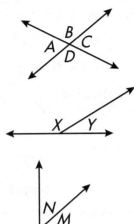

Two angles are **supplementary** if their sum is 180°. In the figure, ∠X and ∠Y are supplementary angles. The measure of ∠X = 150° and the measure of ∠Y = 30°. If two angles have a common vertex and their sides form a straight line, they are supplementary because a straight line has an angle measure of 180°.

Two angles are **complementary** if their sum is 90°. In the figure, ∠M and ∠N are complementary. The measure of ∠M is 40° and the measure of ∠N is 50°.

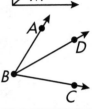

An **angle bisector** is a line drawn through the vertex of an angle that divides it into two congruent angles, or angles that have the same measure. In the figure, ray *BD* bisects ∠ABC so that the measure of ∠ABD is the same as the measure of ∠DBC.

Identify each pair of angles as supplementary or vertical.

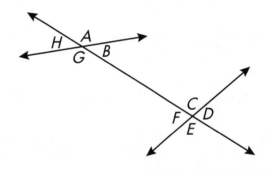

1. ∠A and ∠G _____

2. ∠B and ∠G _____

3. ∠C and ∠D _____

4. ∠C and ∠E _____

5. ∠H and ∠B _____

6. ∠F and ∠E _____

Solve each problem.

7. ∠A and ∠G are vertical angles. The measure of ∠A is 72°, what is the measure of ∠G? _____

8. ∠Y and ∠Z are supplementary angles. The measure of ∠Y is 112°. What is the measure

   of ∠Z? _____

9. ∠A and ∠B are complementary angles. The measure of ∠A is 53°. What is the measure

   of ∠B? _____

10. ∠RST is bisected by ray *SW*. The measure of ∠WST is 30°, what

    is the measure of ∠RST? _____

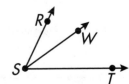

Lesson 12.4 Triangles

A **triangle** is a three-sided figure. The sum of the measures of a triangle is 180°. Triangles are classified by their angles in three categories.

acute triangle	right triangle	obtuse triangle
Acute angles are greater than 0° and less than 90°.	This symbol indicates a **right angle**. Right angles equal 90°.	**Obtuse angles** are greater than 90°. 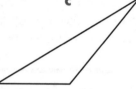
3 acute angles	1 right angle	1 obtuse angle

Identify each triangle below as acute, right, or obtuse.

	a	b	c
1.	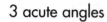 _____	_____	_____
2.	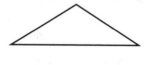 _____	_____	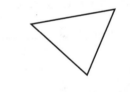 _____
3.	_____	_____	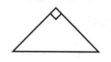 _____
4.	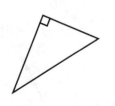 _____	_____	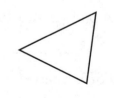 _____

NAME _____

Lesson 12.5 Quadrilaterals

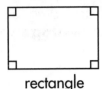   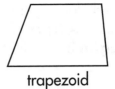 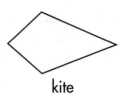

rectangle   square   rhombus   trapezoid   kite

A **rectangle** has four right angles, two pairs of parallel sides, and two pairs of congruent sides.

A **square** is a rectangle with four congruent sides.

A **rhombus** has two pairs of parallel sides and four congruent sides.

A square is a special kind of rectangle and also a special kind of rhombus.

A **trapezoid** has only one pair of parallel sides.

A **kite** has two pairs of congruent sides but no parallel sides.

Use the figures below to answer each question. Letters may be used more than once. Some questions will have more than one answer. Some letters may not be used.

 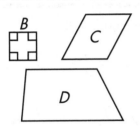 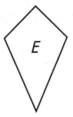 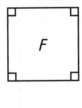 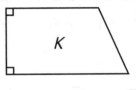   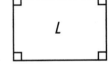

1. Which figure is a rectangle? _____

2. Which figure is a rhombus? _____

3. Which figure is a trapezoid? _____

4. Which figure is a square? _____

5. Which figure is a kite? _____

6. Which figure is both a rhombus and a rectangle? _____

7. Which figures have a right angle? _____

8. Which figures have an obtuse angle? _____

9. Which figures have both a right angle and an obtuse angle? _____

10. Which figures have more than one right angle? _____

11. Which figures have more than one obtuse angle? _____

12. Do any of the figures have four acute angles? _____

Lesson 12.6 Polygons

A **polygon** is a closed plane figure made up of straight lines. Polygons are named according to the number of their sides. A **triangle** has 3 sides. A **quadrilateral** has 4 sides. A **pentagon** has 5 sides. A **hexagon** has 6 sides.

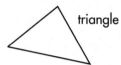 triangle

 quadrilateral

pentagon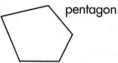

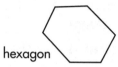 hexagon

Two polygons are congruent if they have exactly the same size and the same shape. Their corresponding sides and their corresponding angles must be congruent. One way to determine if two polygons are congruent is to trace over one of them and match it to the other one. Another way is to measure the corresponding angles and sides.

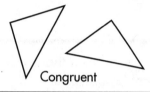 Congruent

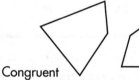 Congruent

Mark each pair of polygons that are congruent with a *C* or not congruent with an *N*.

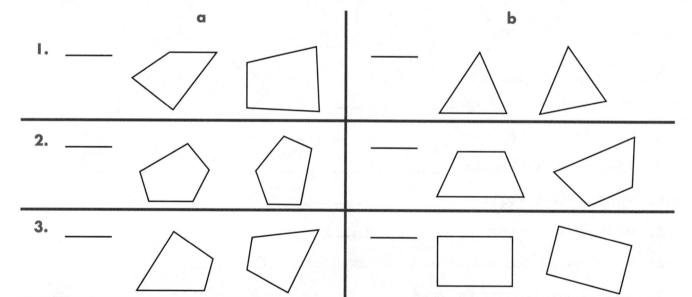

	a	**b**
1. _____		_____
2. _____		_____
3. _____		_____

Measure the angles and sides of each triangle.

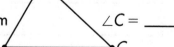

4. $\overline{AB}$ = _____ cm $\angle A$ = _____   7. $\angle D$ = _____ $\overline{DE}$ = _____ cm

5. $\overline{BC}$ = _____ cm $\angle B$ = _____   8. $\angle E$ = _____ $\overline{EF}$ = _____ cm

6. $\overline{AC}$ = _____ cm $\angle C$ = _____   9. $\angle F$ = _____ $\overline{DF}$ = _____ cm

10. Are the triangles congruent? _____

Lesson 12.7 Circles

The **origin** of a circle is a point inside the circle that is the same distance from any point on the circle. A circle is named by its origin.

A **radius** of a circle is a line segment with one endpoint at the origin and the other endpoint on the circle.

A **chord** is a line segment with both endpoints on the circle.

A **diameter** is a chord that passes through the origin of the circle.

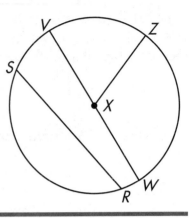

Name a radius, chord, and diameter of circle X.

radius: $\overline{XZ}$, $\overline{XV}$, or $\overline{XW}$ chord: $\overline{VW}$ or $\overline{SR}$ diameter: $\overline{VW}$

---

1. Identify each line segment as radius, chord, or diameter.

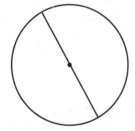 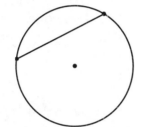  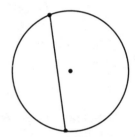

_____ _____ _____ _____

Use the figure at the right to answer the questions.

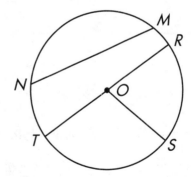

2. Name the circle. _____

3. Name the origin. _____

4. Name a radius. _____

5. Name a chord. _____

6. Name a diameter. _____

7. Draw a circle F, with radius $\overline{FG}$, diameter $\overline{HK}$, and chord $\overline{LM}$.

Lesson 12.8 Solid Figures

A **solid figure** is a three-dimensional figure. A **face** is a flat surface of a solid figure. An **edge** is the intersection of two faces. A **vertex** is a point where three or more faces meet. A **base** is a face on which the solid figure rests.

 A **cube** has 6 square faces.

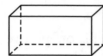 A **rectangular solid** has 6 rectangular faces.

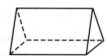 A **triangular solid** has 2 triangular faces and 3 rectangular faces

 A **triangular pyramid** has 4 triangular faces.

 A **square pyramid** has 1 square base and 4 triangular faces.

 A **cone** has a circular base and 1 vertex.

 A **cylinder** has 2 circular bases.

Name each figure.

1. A _____   4. D _____

2. B _____   5. E _____

3. C _____   6. F _____

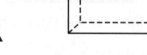

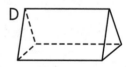

For the figures above, fill in the missing information.

	Number of Faces	Number of Edges	Number of Vertices
7. A	_____	_____	_____
8. B	_____	_____	_____
9. C	_____	_____	_____
10. D	_____	_____	_____
11. E			_____
12. F		_____	_____

Check What You Learned

Geometry

Identify each of the following and name it.

1. A B _____ _____   R S _____ _____

2. C D _____ _____   J K _____ _____

3. E F _____ _____   L M _____ _____

Name the angles and tell if they are acute (A), obtuse (O), or right (R). Measure them.

4.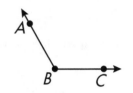

_____   _____   _____

_____   _____   _____

_____   _____   _____

Complete the equations below.

$\angle A = 50°$, $\angle X = 65°$

5. $\angle B =$ _____

6. $\angle C =$ _____

7. $\angle D =$ _____

8. $\angle Y =$ _____

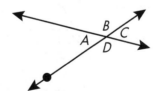 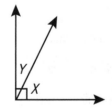

Identify the triangles as acute (A), obtuse (O), or right (R).

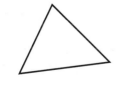 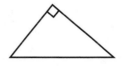 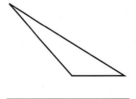

9. _____   _____   _____

Check What You Learned

Geometry

Use the circle to answer the questions.

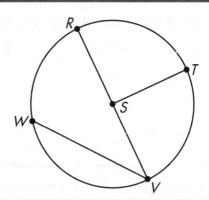

10. Name the circle. _____

11. Name the origin of the circle. _____

12. Name a radius. _____

13. Name a diameter. _____

14. Name a chord that is not a diameter. _____

Complete.

15. Write if the following pairs of polygons are congruent (C) or not congruent (N).

   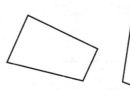

_____   _____

Match each term with its picture. You may use a letter more than once. A question may have more than one answer.

16. cube   _____

17. triangular solid   _____

18. triangular pyramid _____

19. rectangular solid _____

20. square pyramid   _____

21. trapezoid   _____

22. kite   _____

23. cylinder   _____

24. rhombus   _____

25. cone   _____

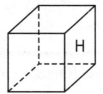 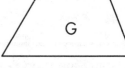

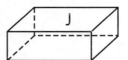 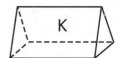

Check What You Know

Preparing for Algebra

Find the value of each expression.

a	b	c
1. $4 \times (8 - 3)$ _____	$4 + 5 \times 3 - 6$ _____	$16 - 4 \times 2$ _____
2. $25 \div 5 + 12 \div 4$ _____	$6 \times 2 \div 4 - 1$ _____	$(40 \div 8) \times 3$ _____

Name the property shown by each statement.

3. $5 \times 6 = 6 \times 5$ _____ $2 \times (3 \times 4) = (2 \times 3) \times 4$ _____ $0 \times 7 = 0$ _____

4. $56 \times 1 = 56$ _____ $44 + 39 = 39 + 44$ _____ $25 + 0 = 25$ _____

Rewrite each expression using the Distributive Property.

5. $4 \times (6 + 2) =$ _____ $(2 \times 5) + (2 \times 4) =$ _____ $4 \times (2 + 6) =$ _____

Replace a with 3, b with 4, and c with 2. Then, find the value of each expression.

6. $a \times (b + c) =$ _____ $(c \times a) + (c \times b) =$ _____ $b \times (a + c) =$ _____

Identify each of the following as an expression or an equation.

7. $5 + x$ _____ $6 + 4 = 10$ _____ $75 \times n$ _____

For each term below, identify the coefficient (C) and the variable (V).

8. $5y$ C _____ V _____ $2x$ C _____ V _____ n C _____ V _____

Use the number line to help answer the questions about integers.

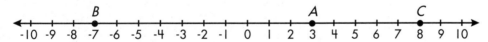

Use integers to name each point on the number line.

9. A _____   B _____   C _____

Use one of the two symbols > or < to compare each pair of numbers.

10. 2 _____ 7   −1 _____ −4   5 _____ 0

Add.

11. $-7 + 4$ _____ $-2 + (-5)$ _____ $-3 + 3$ _____

Check What You Know

Preparing for Algebra

Solve each equation.

	a	b	c
12.	$x - 4 = 4$ _____	$x + 3 = 5$ _____	$n - 2 = 0$ _____
13.	$b + 8 = 19$ _____	$n + 5 = 5$ _____	$y + 3 = 3$ _____
14.	$a + 4 = 11$ _____	$n - 8 = 8$ _____	$y - 5 = 5$ _____
15.	$\frac{a}{4} = 4$ _____	$a \times 4 = 4$ _____	$\frac{m}{5} = 5$ _____
16.	$y \times 20 = 30$ _____	$\frac{x}{12} = 3$ _____	$b \times 7 = 21$ _____
17.	$\frac{x}{5} = 20$ _____	$n \times 5 = 25$ _____	$\frac{x}{9} = 1$ _____

Write each power as a product of factors.

18. 2^4 _____ 9^2 _____ 5^3 _____

Use exponents to write these numbers.

19. $4 \times 4 \times 4 \times 4$ _____ $2 \times 2 \times 2$ _____ $6 \times 6 \times 6 \times 6 \times 6$ _____

Evaluate each expression.

20. x^4 if $x = 3$ _____ b^3 if $b = 5$ _____ y^7 if $y = 1$ _____

Name the point for each ordered pair, and find the ordered pair for each point.

	a	b
21.	(1, 7) _____	F _____
22.	(9, 6) _____	K _____
23.	(2, 8) _____	H _____
24.	(4, 4) _____	G _____
25.	(1, 3) _____	L _____

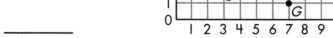

Lesson 13.1 The Order of Operations

The **order of operations** is used to find the value of an expression with more than one operation.

1. Do all operations within parentheses.
2. Do all multiplications and divisions in order, from left to right.
3. Do all additions and subtractions in order from left to right.

$3 \times (4 + 5) + 6 \div 3$	Do the operation inside the parentheses.
$3 \times 9 + 6 \div 3$	Multiply and divide from left to right.
$27 + 2$	Add.
29	

Name the operation that should be done first.

	a	b	c
1.	$7 \times 3 + 2$ _____	$2 + 3 \times 5$ _____	$4 + 3 - 5$ _____
2.	$8 - 6 + 4$ _____	$7 + 9 \div 3$ _____	$12 \div 3 \times 5$ _____
3.	$(3 + 5) \times (3 + 1)$ _____	$(5 - 3) \div 2$ _____	$(2 + 5) \times 3$ _____

Find the value of each expression.

	a	b
4.	$5 \times (5 - 3)$ _____	$5 + 4 \times 3 + 6$ _____
5.	$20 - 4 \times 3$ _____	$(32 \div 8) \times 2$ _____
6.	$15 \div 3 + 16 \div 4$ _____	$4 \times 3 \div 6 - 1$ _____
7.	$20 \div 5 \times 2$ _____	$(7 \times 8) - (4 \times 9)$ _____
8.	$6 \times 5 - 5 \times 4$ _____	$84 \div (8 + 6) \div 3$ _____
9.	$(7 - 3) \times 2$ _____	$16 \div (8 - 6)$ _____
10.	$(2 \times 5) \times 4$ _____	$2 \times (5 \times 4)$ _____
11.	$8 - (5 + 2)$ _____	$(8 - 5) + 2$ _____
12.	$4 \times (5 + 3)$ _____	$(4 \times 5) + (4 \times 3)$ _____

Lesson 13.2 Number Properties

There are certain rules or properties of math that are always true.
The **Commutative Properties** of addition and multiplication state that the order in which numbers are added or multiplied does not change the result.

$a + b = b + a$ and $a \times b = b \times a$
$2 + 3 = 5$ $5 \times 2 = 10$
$3 + 2 = 5$ $2 \times 5 = 10$

The **Associative Properties** of addition and multiplication state that the way in which addends or factors are grouped does not change the result.

$(a + b) + c = a + (b + c)$ and $(a \times b) \times c = a \times (b \times c)$
$(2 + 3) + 4 = 2 + (3 + 4)$ $(2 \times 4) \times 5 = 2 \times (4 \times 5)$
$5 + 4$ $2 + 7$ 8×5 2×20
9 9 40 40

The **Identity Property of Addition** states that the sum of an addend and 0 is the addend.
$5 + 0 = 5$

The **Identity Property of Multiplication** states that the product of a factor and 1 is that factor. $4 \times 1 = 4$

The **Properties of Zero** state that the product of a factor and 0 is 0. $5 \times 0 = 0$

The properties of zero also state that the quotient of zero and any non-zero divisor is 0. $0 \div 5 = 0$

Name the property shown by each statement.

	a	b
1.	$2 \times 8 = 8 \times 2$ _____	$2 + (3 + 4) = (2 + 3) + 4$ _____
2.	$35 \times 1 = 35$ _____	$32 + 25 = 25 + 32$ _____
3.	$4 \times (6 \times 2) = (4 \times 6) \times 2$ _____	$0 \times 9 = 0$ _____
4.	$45 + 0 = 45$ _____	$18 \times 0 = 0 \times 18$ _____

Rewrite each expression using the property indicated.

5. Associative; $(3 + 5) + 2 =$ _____   Commutative; $5 \times 7 =$ _____

6. Identity; $0 + 4 =$ _____   Associative; $3 \times (2 \times 5) =$ _____

7. Commutative; $7 + 9 =$ _____   Associative; $(2 + 5) + 4 =$ _____

8. Identity; $7 \times 1 =$ _____   Identity; $37 + 0 =$ _____

9. Properties of Zero; $0 \times 12 =$ _____   Properties of Zero; $0 \div 6 =$ _____

Lesson 13.3 The Distributive Property

The **Distributive Property** combines the operations of addition and multiplication.

$$a \times (b + c) \qquad = \qquad (a \times b) + (a \times c)$$
$$3 \times (2 + 5) \qquad\qquad (3 \times 2) + (3 \times 5)$$
$$3 \times 7 \qquad\qquad\qquad 6 \ + \ 15$$
$$21 \qquad\qquad\qquad\qquad 21$$

Indicate which operation should be done first.

	a	b

1. $(2 \times 5) + (2 \times 3)$ _____ $7 \times (3 + 5)$ _____

2. $(6 + 9) \times 4$ _____ $(3 \times 5) + (3 \times 7)$ _____

Rewrite each expression using the Distributive Property.

3. $4 \times (6 + 2) =$ _____ $(2 \times 5) + (2 \times 4) =$ _____

4. $(5 \times 1) + (5 \times 6) =$ _____ $4 \times (2 + 6) =$ _____

5. $8 \times (4 + 3) =$ _____ $(5 \times 0) + (5 \times 1) =$ _____

Write each missing number.

6. $(5 \times 3) + (n \times 4) = 5 \times (3 + 4)$ _____ $7 \times (n + 3) = (7 \times 2) + (7 \times 3)$ _____

7. $n \times (5 + 3) = (6 \times 5) + (6 \times 3)$ _____ $(5 \times 7) + (n \times 4) = 5 \times (7 + 4)$ _____

8. $(4 \times 5) + (4 \times 2) = 4 \times (5 + n)$ _____ $3 \times (n + 5) = (3 \times 4) + (3 \times 5)$ _____

Replace a with 2, b with 5, and c with 3. Then, find the value of each expression

9. $a \times (b + c) =$ _____ $(a \times b) + (a \times c) =$ _____

10. $(c \times a) + (c \times b) =$ _____ $b \times (a + c) =$ _____

Lesson 13.4 Variable Expressions and Equations

A **variable** is a symbol, usually a letter of the alphabet, that stands for an unknown number, or quantity. a = variable

An **algebraic expression** is a combination of numbers, variables, and at least one operation. $x + 13$

A **term** is a number, variable, product, or quotient in an algebraic expression. In $3a + 5$, $3a$ is a term and 5 also is a term.

The term $3a$ means $3 \times a$. The number 3 is the coefficient of a. A **coefficient** is a number that multiplies a variable.

In the expression $x + 5$, the coefficient of x is understood to be 1.

An **equation** is a sentence that contains an equal sign. $x + 13 = 25$

Identify each of the following as an expression or an equation.

	a	b	c

1. $3 + x$ _____ $7 + 4 = 11$ _____ $55 \times n$ _____

2. $x - 7 = 15$ _____ $b - 45$ _____ $24 = 6 \times 4$ _____

For each term below, identify the coefficient and the variable.

  a   b

3. $3x$ coefficient _____ variable _____ $4y$ coefficient _____ variable _____

4. z coefficient _____ variable _____ $5n$ coefficient _____ variable _____

5. $7b$ coefficient _____ variable _____ m coefficient _____ variable _____

6. r coefficient _____ variable _____ $6d$ coefficient _____ variable _____

Translate each phrase into an algebraic expression.

7. five more than n _____   eight decreased by x _____

8. x added to seven _____   the product of n and 11 _____

Translate each sentence into an equation.

9. Six times a number is 18. _____   Seventy less a number is 29. _____

10. Eight divided by a number is 2. _____   The product of 7 and 12 is 84. _____

Write the following expressions in words.

11. $6 - n = 3$ _____

12. $5 \times 13 = 65$ _____

Lesson 13.5 Solving Addition and Subtraction Equations

Subtraction Property of Equality

If you subtract the same number from each side of an equation, the two sides remain equal.

$$x + 12 = 20$$

To undo the addition of 12, subtract 12.

$$x + 12 - 12 = 20 - 12$$
$$x + 0 = 8$$
$$x = 8$$

Addition Property of Equality

If you add the same number to each side of an equation, the two sides remain equal.

$$n - 3 = 15$$

To undo the subtraction of 3, add 3.

$$n - 3 + 3 = 15 + 3$$
$$n - 0 = 12$$
$$n = 12$$

Write the operation that would undo the operation in the equation.

a	b
1. $x - 4 = 3$ _____	$8 = b + 4$ _____
2. $y + 7 = 25$ _____	$3 = a - 7$ _____

Solve each equation.

a	b	c
3. $a - 4 = 2$ _____	$y + 5 = 9$ _____	$x - 3 = 14$ _____
4. $7 = x - 4$ _____	$b + 7 = 19$ _____	$y + 5 = 5$ _____
5. $z - 7 = 5$ _____	$m - 5 = 5$ _____	$n + 1 = 1$ _____
6. $x + 7 = 10$ _____	$x - 3 = 18$ _____	$x + 0 = 9$ _____
7. $b + 4 = 4$ _____	$b - 8 = 12$ _____	$n + 8 = 12$ _____
8. $z - 10 = 20$ _____	$z + 5 = 20$ _____	$x - 2 = 8$ _____

SHOW YOUR WORK

Write and solve the equation for each problem below.

9. Kelley went to the movies. She took 20 dollars with her. When she came home, she had 6 dollars. How much money did she spend? _____

9.

10. There are 27 students in Mrs. Yuen's homeroom. Twelve of them have home computers. How many students do not have home computers?

_____

10.

Lesson 13.6 Solving Multiplication and Division Equations

Division Property of Equality
If you divide each side of an equation by the same nonzero number, the two sides remain equal.

$$3 \times y = 21$$

To undo multiplication by 3, divide by 3.

$$\frac{3 \times y}{3} = \frac{21}{3}$$
$$y = 7$$

Multiplication Property of Equality
If you multiply each side of an equation by the same number, the two sides remain equal.

$$\frac{a}{4} = 5$$

To undo division by 4, multiply by 4.

$$\frac{a}{4} \times \frac{4}{1} = 5 \times 4$$
$$a = 20$$

Write the operation that would undo the operation in each equation.

	a	b
1.	$5 \times n = 40$ _____	$\frac{y}{5} = 80$ _____
2.	$\frac{x}{2} = 8$ _____	$a \times 7 = 42$ _____

Solve each equation.

	a	b	c
3.	$3 \times a = 9$ _____	$\frac{x}{5} = 5$ _____	$\frac{n}{4} = 3$ _____
4.	$\frac{x}{3} = 3$ _____	$n \times 4 = 4$ _____	$3 \times y = 24$ _____
5.	$5 \times b = 10$ _____	$\frac{b}{8} = 2$ _____	$4 \times a = 20$ _____
6.	$\frac{m}{3} = 1$ _____	$8 \times n = 20$ _____	$\frac{x}{5} = 2$ _____
7.	$4 \times n = 1$ _____	$\frac{n}{4} = 5$ _____	$\frac{b}{3} = 27$ _____
8.	$n \times 15 = 30$ _____	$\frac{n}{4} = 10$ _____	$n \times 12 = 36$ _____
9.	$\frac{n}{18} = 2$ _____	$n \times 3 = 18$ _____	$n \times 2 = 20$ _____
10.	$\frac{n}{2} = 20$ _____	$\frac{n}{16} = 1$ _____	$n \times 3 = 3$ _____
11.	$5 \times b = 30$ _____	$\frac{b}{5} = 30$ _____	$n \times 8 = 24$ _____
12.	$\frac{n}{4} = 1$ _____	$\frac{b}{2} = 2$ _____	$n \times 6 = 48$ _____

Lesson 13.7 Exponents and Scientific Notation

A **power** of a number represents repeated multiplication of the number by itself.
$10^3 = 10 \times 10 \times 10$ and is read 10 to the third power.

In **exponential** numbers, the **base** is the number that is multiplied, and the **exponent** represents the number of times the base is used as a factor. In 10^3, 10 is the base and 3 is the exponent.

2^5 means 2 is used as a factor 5 times.
$2 \times 2 \times 2 \times 2 \times 2 = 32$ $2^5 = 32$

Scientific notation for a number is expressed by writing the number as the product of a number greater than or equal to one, but less than ten and a power of ten.

3000 can be written as 3×1000 or 3×10^3.
3×10^3 is scientific notation for 3000.

Some powers of 10 are shown in the table at right.

10^1	10	10
10^2	10×10	100
10^3	$10 \times 10 \times 10$	1000
10^4	$10 \times 10 \times 10 \times 10$	10000
10^5	$10 \times 10 \times 10 \times 10 \times 10$	100000

Use the table above to write these numbers in scientific notation.

	a	b	c
1.	30 _____	4,000 _____	50,000 _____
2.	600,000 _____	700 _____	90 _____
3.	40,000 _____	100,000 _____	400 _____

Write each power as the product of factors.

4.	3^3 _____	5^5 _____	1^6 _____
5.	12^2 _____	8^3 _____	6^3 _____
6.	7^4 _____	4^4 _____	11^4 _____

Use exponents to write these numbers.

7.	$3 \times 3 \times 3$ ____	8×8 ____	$7 \times 7 \times 7 \times 7 \times 7$ ____
8.	24×24 ____	$4 \times 4 \times 4$ ____	$6 \times 6 \times 6 \times 6 \times 6 \times 6$ ____
9.	$2 \times 2 \times 2 \times 2$ ____	$38 \times 38 \times 38$ ____	$5 \times 5 \times 5 \times 5 \times 5$ ____

Evaluate each expression.

10.	a^4 if $a = 2$ ____	x^3 if $x = 4$ ____	n^7 if $n = 1$ ____
11.	n^2 if $n = 8$ ____	b^4 if $b = 3$ ____	x^3 if $x = 5$ ____
12.	a^5 if $a = 3$ ____	x^3 if $x = 6$ ____	n^2 if $n = 11$ ____

Lesson 13.8 Comparing and Ordering Integers

Integers are the set of whole numbers and their opposites.

Positive integers are greater than zero. **Negative integers** are less than zero. Zero is neither positive nor negative. A negative integer is less than a positive integer. On a number line, an integer and its opposite are the same distance from zero. The smaller of two integers is always the one to the left on a number line.

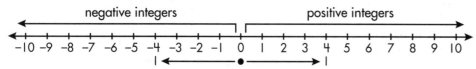

The opposite of 4 is −4. They are both 4 spaces from 0.

$$-7 < -2$$
−7 is to the left of −2.

$$-4 > -9$$
−4 is to the right of −9.

Use integers to name each point on the number line.

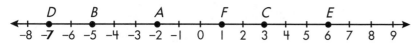

a	b	c
1. A _____	D _____	F _____
2. E _____	C _____	B _____

Use one of the two symbols, > or <, to compare each pair of numbers.

3. 2 _____ 7   −1 _____ −4   5 _____ 0

4. −4 _____ 1   0 _____ −8   −8 _____ −10

5. 7 _____ −7   −2 _____ 0   4 _____ 6

6. 1 _____ −1   6 _____ 3   −6 _____ −3

7. 4 _____ −2   −6 _____ −4   3 _____ −3

List in order from smallest to largest.

       a   b

8. −3, −5, 0 _____   8, −8, 2 _____

9. 0, 5, −3, −7 _____   4, −1, 2, −2 _____

10. −6, 5, −2, −3, 2 _____   5, −8, −2, −3, 0 _____

NAME _____

Lesson 13.9 Adding Integers

The sum of two positive integers is a positive integer.

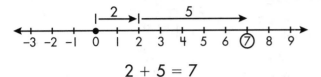

$$2 + 5 = 7$$

The sum of two negative integers is a negative integer.

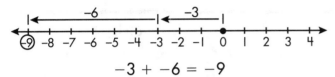

$$-3 + -6 = -9$$

To find the sum of two integers with opposite signs, subtract the digit of lesser value from the digit of greater value and keep the sign of the greater digit.

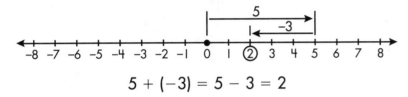

$$5 + (-3) = 5 - 3 = 2$$

Add.

	a	b	c	d
1.	3 + 4 _____	−3 + (−4) _____	3 + (−4) _____	−3 + 4 _____
2.	−3 + (−3) _____	3 + (−3) _____	−3 + 3 _____	3 + 3 _____
3.	5 + (−1) _____	−5 + 1 _____	−5 + (−1) _____	5 + 1 _____
4.	−7 + 3 _____	−7 + (−3) _____	7 + (−3) _____	7 + 3 _____
5.	4 + 7 _____	4 + (−7) _____	−4 + (7) _____	−4 + (−7) _____
6.	8 + (−8) _____	−8 + (−8) _____	8 + 8 _____	−8 + 8 _____
7.	−3 + 0 _____	3 + 0 _____	−5 + (−6) _____	−5 + 6 _____
8.	5 + (−6) _____	5 + 6 _____	−8 + 0 _____	8 + 0 _____
9.	−3 + 6 _____	−3 + (−6) _____	3 + 6 _____	3 + (−6) _____
10.	−6 + (−4) _____	−6 + 4 _____	6 + (−4) _____	6 + 4 _____

Lesson 13.10 Plotting Ordered Pairs

The position of any point on a grid can be described by an ordered pair of numbers. The two numbers are named in order: (x, y). Point A on the grid at the right is named by the ordered pair (3, 2). It is located at 3 on the horizontal scale (x) and at 2 on the vertical scale (y). The number on the horizontal scale is always named first in an ordered pair. Point B is named by the ordered pair (7, 3).

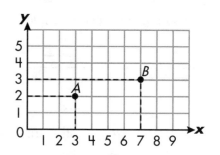

Use Grid 1 to name the point for each ordered pair.

Grid 1

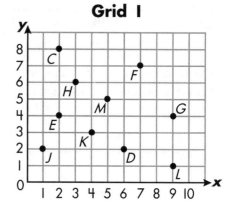

1. (1, 2) _____   (2, 4) _____

2. (3, 6) _____   (9, 4) _____

3. (9, 1) _____   (5, 5) _____

4. (2, 8) _____   (4, 3) _____

5. (7, 7) _____   (6, 2) _____

Use Grid 2 to find the ordered pair for each labeled point.

Grid 2

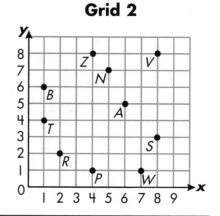

6. B _____   V _____

7. S _____   A _____

8. W _____   N _____

9. T _____   R _____

10. Z _____   P _____

Plot the four points shown on Grid 3. Label the points.

Grid 3

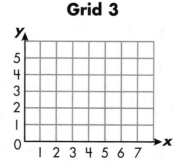

       a   b

11. A (2, 4)   D (3, 5)

12. C (5, 1)   Z (6, 3)

Check What You Learned

Preparing for Algebra

Find the value of each expression.

	a	**b**	**c**
1.	$2 \times (7 - 3)$ _____	$3 + 4 \times 2 - 5$ _____	$12 - 4 \times 3$ _____
2.	$20 \div 5 + 16 \div 4$ _____	$7 \times 6 \div 3 - 1$ _____	$(45 \div 9) \times 2$ _____

Name the property shown by each statement.

3. $7 \times 2 = 2 \times 7$ _____ $3 \times (5 \times 4) = (3 \times 5) \times 4$ _____ $0 \times 8 = 0$ _____

4. $36 \times 1 = 36$ _____ $24 + 19 = 19 + 24$ _____ $55 + 0 = 55$ _____

Rewrite each expression using the Distributive Property.

5. $3 \times (5 + 1) =$ _____ $(4 \times 6) + (4 \times 5) =$ _____ $7 \times (3 + 6) =$ _____

Replace a with 4, b with 2, and c with 5. Then find the value of each expression.

6. $a \times (b + c) =$ _____ $(c \times a) + (c \times b) =$ _____ $b \times (a + c) =$ _____

Identify each of the following as an expression or an equation.

7. $7 + x$ _____ $9 + 4 = 13$ _____ $85 \times n$ _____

For each term below, identify the coefficient (C) and the variable (V).

8. $9y$ C _____ V _____ $4b$ C _____ V _____ m C _____ V _____

Use the number line to help answer the questions about integers.

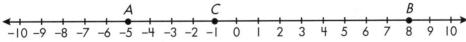

Use integers to name each point on the number line.

9. A _____ B _____ C _____

Use one of the two symbols > or < to compare each pair of numbers.

10. 3 _____ 9 -9 _____ -4 -5 _____ 0

Add.

11. $-8 + 5$ _____ $-3 + (-5)$ _____ $-8 + 8$ _____

Check What You Learned

Preparing for Algebra

Solve each equation.

	a	b	c
12.	$x - 5 = 3$ _____	$x + 5 = 8$ _____	$y - 4 = 0$ _____
13.	$x - 19 = 8$ _____	$x - 12 = 4$ _____	$n + 8 = 8$ _____
14.	$b - 7 = 0$ _____	$n + 3 = 3$ _____	$x + 2 = 8$ _____
15.	$\frac{x}{3} = 3$ _____	$n \times 5 = 5$ _____	$\frac{b}{2} = 1$ _____
16.	$b \times 8 = 12$ _____	$\frac{x}{3} = 8$ _____	$a \times 2 = 3$ _____
17.	$\frac{n}{4} = 4$ _____	$n \times 8 = 8$ _____	$b \times 3 = 18$ _____

Write each power as a product of factors.

18. 3^5 _____ 12^2 _____ 6^4 _____

Use exponents to write these numbers.

19. $2 \times 2 \times 2 \times 2 \times 2$ _____ $8 \times 8 \times 8$ _____ 25×25 _____

Evaluate each expression.

20. x^4 if $x = 2$ _____ b^3 if $b = 7$ _____ x^3 if $x = 3$ _____

Name the point for each ordered pair, and find the ordered pair for each point.

	a	b
21.	(6, 7) _____	F _____
22.	(10, 5) _____	G _____
23.	(8, 3) _____	K _____
24.	(1, 8) _____	H _____
25.	(2, 4) _____	L _____

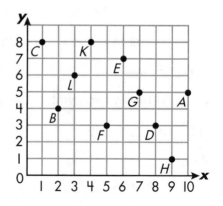

Final Test Chapters 1–13

Complete as indicated.

	a	**b**	**c**	**d**
1.	238 463 +519	4763 −2188	248 × 32	432 ×218

2.

0.687
8.9
+3.925

10.65
− 2.319

68.3
× 7.24

0.89)‾3.8448

Estimate.

3.

588
+407

874
−223

385
×   8

615
× 28

Complete as indicated. Give answers in simplest form.

4. $\frac{3}{5}$
$+\frac{2}{3}$

$4\frac{1}{3}$
$-2\frac{3}{4}$

$\frac{2}{3} \times 2\frac{1}{4}$

$\frac{4}{5} \div \frac{2}{3}$

Find the least common multiple (LCM) and greatest common factor (GCF).

5.   8 and 12

LCM _____

GCF _____

3 and 7

LCM _____

GCF _____

4 and 8

LCM _____

GCF _____

12 and 18

LCM _____

GCF _____

Final Test Chapters 1–13

Complete the following.

	a	b	c	d
6.	83% of 6 = _____	34% of 25 = _____	125% of 80 = _____	4% of 37 = _____

Complete as indicated.

7.

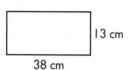

13 cm

38 cm

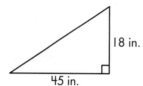

18 in.

45 in.

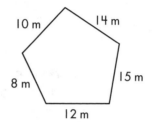

10 m   14 m

8 m   15 m

12 m

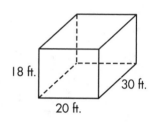

18 ft.   30 ft.

20 ft.

area =

_____ sq. cm

area =

_____ sq. in.

perimeter =

_____ m

volume =

_____ cu. ft.

Use the circle to answer the questions.

8. Name the circle. _____

9. The origin of the circle is _____.

10. A radius of the circle is _____.

11. A diameter of the circle is _____.

12. Specify a chord that is not a diameter _____.

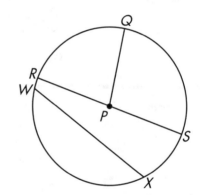

Answer the questions about the angles below. ∠m = 55°, ∠x = 35°

13. ∠Y = _____

14. ∠Z = _____

15. ∠W = _____

16. ∠N = _____

17. Which ∠s are obtuse? _____

18. Which ∠s are acute? _____

19. Which ∠ is right? _____

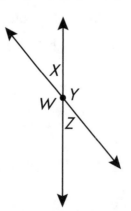

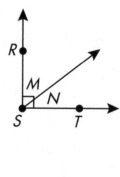

Final Test Chapters 1–13

Complete as indicated.

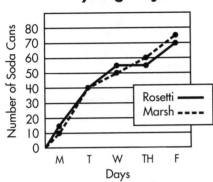

Results of Recycling Project

Number of Soda Cans — 0 10 20 30 40 50 60 70 80

Rosetti ———
Marsh ----

M T W TH F
Days

Mr. Rosetti's homeroom and Ms. Marsh's homeroom collected soda cans for a week-long recycling project. The results are shown on the line graph at the left.

20. On Monday, which homeroom collected the most cans? _____

21. On what day had each homeroom collected the same number of cans? _____

22. On what day did Mr. Rosetti's homeroom collect no cans? _____

23. What was the total number of cans collected? _____

---

24. Draw a stem and leaf plot for the following set of numbers.
45, 37, 45, 52, 47, 33, 54, 47, 36, 41, 47

Find the mean, median, mode, and range for the numbers at the left.

mean _____

median _____

mode _____

range _____

Solve these equations.

	a	**b**	**c**
25.	$x - 5 = 4$ _____	$x + 6 = 10$ _____	$x - 7 = 0$ _____
26.	$x - 17 = 8$ _____	$x - 10 = 0$ _____	$x + 9 = 9$ _____
27.	$a \times 4 = 6$ _____	$a \times 3 = 9$ _____	$a \times 2 = 1$ _____
28.	$\frac{a}{2} = 4$ _____	$\frac{a}{3} = 1$ _____	$\frac{a}{7} = 2$ _____

Name the point for each ordered pair.

29. (6, 4) _____

30. (1, 8) _____

31. (9, 1) _____

32. (1, 4) _____

33. (3, 5) _____

Find the ordered pair for each point.

34. F _____

35. G _____

36. K _____

37. H _____

38. L _____

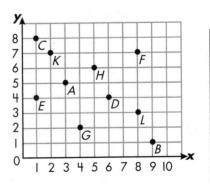

Spectrum Math
Grade 6

Final Test
Chapters 1–13

167

CHAPTERS 1–13 FINAL TEST

Final Test Chapters 1–13

Solve each problem.

39. South Valley Middle School has 1,275 students. North Valley Middle School has 1,181 students. How many students do the schools have combined?

Together the two schools have _____ students.

South Valley has _____ more students than North Valley.

39.

40. Christopher has $2\frac{3}{4}$ pounds of candy. He gave $\frac{2}{5}$ of it to Taylor. How many pounds of candy did Christopher give to Taylor?

Christopher gave _____ of candy to Taylor.

40.

41. Danielle has $4\frac{3}{8}$ yards of ribbon. She cut off a piece of ribbon $2\frac{3}{4}$ yards long and gave it to Adriana. How much ribbon does Danielle have left?

Danielle has _____ yards of ribbon left.

41.

42. The sixth-grade classes at East Side Middle School bought a flag for every classroom in the school. They spent $350.90. Each flag cost $15.95. How many flags did they buy?

They bought flags for _____ classrooms.

42.

43. The municipal swimming pool is 50 meters long, 25 meters wide, and is filled to a uniform depth of 3 meters. What is the volume of water in the pool?

The volume of water is _____ cubic meters.

43.

44. Julia has 3 red marbles, 4 blue marbles, 3 yellow marbles, and 6 black marbles in a bag. She takes one marble out of the bag at random.

The probability that it is a black marble is _____.

The probability that it is a yellow marble is _____.

The probability that it is not a red marble is _____.

44.

45. Malik got 28 questions correct out of 35 on a recent test. What percentage did Malik get correct?

Malik got _____ correct.

45.

Scoring Record for Posttests, Mid-Test, and Final Test

Chapter Posttest	Your Score	Performance			
		Excellent	Very Good	Fair	Needs Improvement
1	____ of 41	39–41	34–38	26–33	25 or fewer
2	____ of 36	34–36	30–33	23–29	22 or fewer
3	____ of 35	34–35	29–33	22–28	21 or fewer
4	____ of 28	26–28	23–26	18–22	17 or fewer
5	____ of 39	37–39	32–36	24–31	23 or fewer
6	____ of 37	35–37	31–34	23–30	22 or fewer
7	____ of 30	29–30	25–28	19–24	18 or fewer
8	____ of 42	40–42	35–39	26–34	25 or fewer
9	____ of 34	33–34	28–32	21–27	20 or fewer
10	____ of 38	36–38	31–35	24–30	23 or fewer
11	____ of 26	25–26	22–24	17–21	16 or fewer
12	____ of 45	43–45	37–42	28–36	27 or fewer
13	____ of 73	69–73	59–68	45–58	44 or fewer
Mid-Test	____ of 77	73–77	63–72	47–62	46 or fewer
Final Test	____ of 85	80–85	69–79	52–68	51 or fewer

Record your test score in the Your Score column. See where your score falls in the Performance columns. Your score is based on the total number of required responses. If your score is fair or needs improvement, review the chapter material.

Grade 6 Answers

Chapter 1

Pretest, page 1

	a	b	c	d	e
1.	567	9298	8157	52230	304540
2.	413	237	102	585	89
3.	1829	10408	72274	81989	894223
4.	5783	1193	3874	785	5757
5.	1672	10508	78813	18304	5398
6.	7848	16526	5936	23868	31396
7.	584521	8585	397718	556459	47500
8.	1650	2383	5081	1064	47

Pretest, page 2

9. 1,054; 97 10. 683 11. 258,300; 129,100
12. 20° 13. 172

Lesson 1.1, page 3

	a	b	c	d	e	f
1.	101	452	393	97	326	781
2.	45	45	237	262	56	8
3.	888	202	400	567	125	521
4.	652	14	26	188	135	35
5.	113	969	503	112	115	616
6.	63	673	33	262	61	166

Lesson 1.2, page 4

	a	b	c	d	e
1.	2537	3797	5327	1804	3615
2.	2187	6342	137	162	86
3.	7553	6461	2410	9419	6299
4.	793	1970	2232	3642	80
5.	2060	2683	2124	3536	2560
6.	268	2717	1106	5335	775

Lesson 1.3, page 5

	a	b	c	d	e
1.	24807	46590	18183	57258	34040
2.	23211	44705	22381	74939	17238
3.	282573	521209	199178	673686	287466
4.	16210	11091	35855	1376	14611
5.	652101	751349	344358	887112	598733
6.	355413	175091	287895	223134	620182
7.	107571	62314	336308	475523	81605

Lesson 1.4, page 6

	a	b	c	d	e
1.	40646	294104	81185	4138	61855
2.	84588	29966	8882	99568	7566
3.	24984	99102	1583	11575	560419
4.	16289	79480	3931	28478	114989

Lesson 1.5, page 7

	a	b	c	d	e
1.	1083	5914	3603	52338	142081
2.	494	75	108	644	109
3.	1550	10570	64165	79189	886269
4.	4685	923	2829	5615	6567
5.	1582	11238	77312	21622	5162
6.	8478	27035	9023	24111	13639
7.	638188	54865	358606	556639	174800
8.	1442	1797	4834	1256	71

Lesson 1.6, page 8

	a	b	c	d
1.	130	320	8000	31000
2.	40	300	3000	40000
3.	180	1500	10000	110000
4.	270; 274			
5.	300; 319			

Posttest, page 9

	a	b	c	d	e
1.	813	8857	1965	59450	320319
2.	259	284	118	209	78
3.	884	8015	75441	73665	357320
4.	1436	2759	518	4815	3777
5.	1377	6545	74260	22186	4590
6.	8179	14908	5645	18411	20857
7.	555037	61784	380063	511661	232200

Posttest, page 10

8. 32,800; 32,821 9. 310 10. 315 11. 20
12. 27

Chapter 2

Pretest, page 11

	a	b	c	d	e
1.	528	455	1532	4875	24378
2.	13r1	56r5	218	340r2	625
3.	3276	6399	7776	32112	240975
4.	3r5	5r6	16r10	23	25
5.	82056	137388	128128	471960	1183572
6.	86	152r31	39	2026	1163r13

Pretest, page 12

7. 336 8. 208,800 9. 52 10. 94 11. 12; 18

Grade 6 Answers

Lesson 2.1, page 13

	a	b	c	d	e	f
1.	219	448	385	384	225	582
2.	1638	1560	1946	1712	610	2569
3.	6104	4158	2312	2967	2559	4302
4.	4860	12828	6310	20340	6300	13069
5.	12250	21936	42420	6334	27957	5568
6.	882	16840	2932	7018	3240	891

Lesson 2.2, page 14

	a	b	c	d
1.	672	630	858	3825
2.	12532	2646	22092	8976
3.	8748	13056	11220	49795
4.	113300	86184	227664	284886

Lesson 2.3, page 15

	a	b	c	d
1.	91086	40068	160366	81420
2.	331364	471534	342042	440295
3.	747612	901550	955192	2070672
4.	1430232	603125	972360	2678144

Lesson 2.4, page 16

	a	b	c	d	e
1.	9r3	12r2	4r1	5r7	16r3
2.	46r1	54r1	163r2	96	45r1
3.	504r3	955	2160r2	1140r2	873r6

Lesson 2.5, page 17

	a	b	c	d	e
1.	5r4	2r14	4	4r2	2r14
2.	2r2	7	27r1	32	29r14
3.	30r5	13r23	19r25	26r17	18

Lesson 2.6, page 18

	a	b	c	d	e
1.	110r25	312	115r21	179r2	110
2.	154r20	113	270r2	523	225
3.	1467r1	725	828r40	886	569

Lesson 2.7, page 19

	a	b	c	d
1.	3000	1000	2800	1200
2.	14000	8000	40000	63000
3.	280000	150000	90000	40000
4.	150000	280000	1800000	1800000
5.	80	80	40	50
6.	900	700	500	700

Lesson 2.7, page 20

1. 540; 60 **2.** 40; 30; 1,200 **3.** 560; 80
4. 300; 90; 27,000 **5.** 40; 10 **6.** 690; 230

Posttest, page 21

	a	b	c	d	e
1.	528	504	2514	4770	34484
2.	9r6	54r3	228	472r4	432
3.	2080	6319	7866	53056	158760
4.	3r1	4r10	14r1	28r16	35
5.	77106	57288	303952	744111	1981692
6.	83	185r4	49	1757r20	1158

Posttest, page 22

7. 3,736 **8.** 19,062 **9.** 89 **10.** 102 **11.** 10; 15

Chapter 3

Pretest, page 23

	a	b	c	d	e
1.	p	c	p	c	p
2.	4	1	12	7	15
3.	$\frac{3}{5}$	$\frac{2}{3}$	$\frac{5}{8}$	$\frac{3}{4}$	$\frac{7}{8}$
4.	$\frac{9}{24}, \frac{10}{24}$	$\frac{8}{12}, \frac{9}{12}$	$\frac{3}{12}, \frac{10}{12}$	$\frac{8}{10}, \frac{5}{10}$	$\frac{14}{21}, \frac{15}{21}$

Pretest, page 24

	a	b	c	d	e
5.	$5\frac{2}{5}$	$4\frac{3}{8}$	$2\frac{1}{7}$	$6\frac{1}{4}$	$5\frac{2}{3}$
6.	$\frac{53}{16}$	$\frac{18}{5}$	$\frac{24}{7}$	$\frac{51}{16}$	$\frac{10}{3}$
7.	$6\frac{2}{3}$	$5\frac{4}{5}$	$2\frac{2}{5}$	$3\frac{5}{6}$	$5\frac{1}{4}$

Lesson 3.1, page 25

	a	b	c
1.	c	p	p
2.	p	c	c
3.	2, 3, 3	2, 2, 2, 5	
4.	2, 2, 2, 2, 3	2, 3, 3, 5	

Lesson 3.2, page 26

	a	b	c
1.	1, 2, 4, 8 1, 2, 3, 4, 6, 12	1, 2, 4	4
2.	1, 2, 3, 6 1, 2, 3, 6, 9, 18	1, 2, 3, 6	6
3.	1, 2, 3, 4, 6, 8, 12, 24 3, 5, 15	1, 3	3
4.	1, 2, 4 1, 2, 3, 6	1, 2	2
5.	1, 5 1, 2, 3, 4, 6, 12	1	1
6.	1, 2, 4, 8, 16 1, 2, 3, 4, 6, 12	1, 2, 4	4
7.	1, 3, 5, 15 1, 2, 3, 6, 9, 18	1, 3	3
8.	1, 7 1, 3	1	1

Grade 6 Answers

Lesson 3.3, page 27

	a	b	c
1.	$\frac{2}{3}$	$\frac{3}{8}$	$\frac{5}{8}$
2.	$3\frac{2}{3}$	$5\frac{1}{2}$	$4\frac{3}{4}$
3.	$\frac{7}{8}$	$\frac{5}{6}$	$\frac{2}{5}$
4.	$\frac{4}{15}$	$\frac{7}{12}$	$\frac{5}{6}$
5.	$2\frac{1}{5}$	$1\frac{5}{6}$	$2\frac{3}{4}$
6.	$\frac{3}{5}$	$\frac{4}{7}$	$\frac{1}{2}$

Lesson 3.4, page 28

	a	b	c
1.	$\frac{3}{12}, \frac{8}{12}$	$\frac{15}{40}, \frac{28}{40}$	$\frac{12}{21}, \frac{14}{21}$
2.	$\frac{9}{24}, \frac{4}{24}$	$\frac{4}{6}, \frac{3}{6}$	$\frac{9}{24}, \frac{20}{24}$
3.	$\frac{6}{15}, \frac{5}{15}$	$\frac{5}{16}, \frac{6}{16}$	$\frac{3}{6}, \frac{2}{6}$
4.	$\frac{10}{16}, \frac{3}{16}$	$\frac{8}{20}, \frac{15}{20}$	$\frac{25}{60}, \frac{48}{60}$
5.	$\frac{8}{18}, \frac{9}{18}$	$\frac{21}{24}, \frac{14}{24}$	$\frac{1}{9}, \frac{6}{9}$

Lesson 3.5, page 29

	a	b	c	d
1.	$4\frac{3}{5}$	$3\frac{1}{4}$	$2\frac{1}{7}$	$1\frac{7}{9}$
2.	$4\frac{1}{6}$	$1\frac{2}{3}$	$2\frac{2}{5}$	$3\frac{3}{4}$
3.	$1\frac{7}{10}$	$5\frac{3}{7}$	$2\frac{4}{5}$	$2\frac{2}{3}$
4.	$6\frac{2}{3}$	$1\frac{1}{6}$	$2\frac{1}{2}$	$1\frac{1}{3}$
5.	$1\frac{1}{2}$	$1\frac{2}{5}$	$1\frac{7}{8}$	$3\frac{1}{8}$
6.	$2\frac{3}{4}$	$5\frac{1}{7}$	$1\frac{3}{4}$	$1\frac{3}{5}$

Lesson 3.6, page 30

	a	b	c	d
1.	$\frac{21}{8}$	$\frac{13}{4}$	$\frac{17}{7}$	$\frac{9}{2}$
2.	$\frac{15}{4}$	$\frac{29}{12}$	$\frac{25}{6}$	$\frac{17}{3}$
3.	$\frac{39}{16}$	$\frac{7}{2}$	$\frac{23}{16}$	$\frac{21}{8}$
4.	$\frac{10}{3}$	$\frac{22}{5}$	$\frac{25}{8}$	$\frac{22}{3}$
5.	$\frac{26}{3}$	$\frac{7}{5}$	$\frac{17}{7}$	$\frac{35}{9}$
6.	$\frac{22}{5}$	$\frac{23}{6}$	$\frac{22}{9}$	$\frac{53}{12}$

Lesson 3.7, page 31

	a	b	c	d
1.	$3\frac{3}{4}$	$2\frac{4}{5}$	$1\frac{3}{4}$	$4\frac{2}{3}$
2.	$3\frac{3}{5}$	$6\frac{3}{4}$	$3\frac{1}{3}$	$4\frac{1}{2}$
3.	$4\frac{1}{2}$	$5\frac{2}{3}$	$8\frac{3}{5}$	$7\frac{1}{4}$
4.	$4\frac{1}{2}$	$4\frac{1}{2}$	$7\frac{2}{3}$	$5\frac{1}{3}$
5.	$5\frac{1}{3}$	$5\frac{1}{5}$	$5\frac{1}{7}$	$4\frac{2}{9}$

Lesson 3.8, page 32

1. $2 \times 3 \times 3 \times 5$
2. 4; 1, 2, 4, 7, 14, 28; 1, 2, 4, 8, 16, 32
3. 24; 8, 16, 24, 32; 6, 12, 18, 24, 30
4. $\frac{2}{7}$ 5. $\frac{3}{4}$ 6. $6\frac{1}{3}$

Posttest, page 33

	a	b	c	d	e
1.	p	c	p	c	c
2.	8	7	9	1	3
3.	$\frac{2}{5}$	$\frac{3}{5}$	$\frac{5}{8}$	$\frac{4}{5}$	$\frac{7}{8}$
4.	$\frac{15}{24}, \frac{14}{24}$	$\frac{9}{12}, \frac{2}{12}$	$\frac{9}{15}, \frac{10}{15}$	$\frac{9}{24}, \frac{16}{24}$	$\frac{16}{56}, \frac{35}{56}$

Posttest, page 34

	a	b	c	d	e
5.	$3\frac{3}{8}$	$3\frac{3}{5}$	$3\frac{1}{6}$	$8\frac{3}{4}$	$5\frac{2}{5}$
6.	$\frac{31}{7}$	$\frac{39}{16}$	$\frac{19}{5}$	$\frac{47}{6}$	$\frac{20}{3}$
7.	$4\frac{2}{5}$	$6\frac{5}{7}$	$2\frac{2}{3}$	$3\frac{3}{4}$	$5\frac{1}{4}$

Chapter 4

Pretest, page 35

	a	b	c	d
1.	$1\frac{1}{4}$	$1\frac{2}{5}$	$1\frac{7}{24}$	$\frac{5}{6}$
2.	$\frac{1}{4}$	$\frac{3}{8}$	$\frac{5}{12}$	$\frac{1}{3}$
3.	$4\frac{7}{24}$	$6\frac{1}{12}$	$8\frac{1}{15}$	$10\frac{11}{14}$
4.	$4\frac{13}{24}$	$4\frac{1}{12}$	$1\frac{5}{6}$	$2\frac{2}{5}$
5.	$4\frac{13}{24}$	$6\frac{7}{8}$	$9\frac{7}{12}$	$4\frac{8}{15}$

Pretest, page 36

6. $1\frac{7}{24}; \frac{1}{24}$ 7. $3\frac{5}{6}; 1\frac{1}{6}$ 8. $3\frac{1}{6}$ 9. $1\frac{7}{12}$

Lesson 4.1, page 37

	a	b	c	d	e
1.	$1\frac{2}{5}$	1	$1\frac{1}{3}$	$1\frac{1}{3}$	$1\frac{1}{5}$
2.	$1\frac{1}{7}$	$\frac{2}{3}$	$1\frac{1}{2}$	$1\frac{1}{2}$	$\frac{4}{5}$
3.	$\frac{2}{3}$	$1\frac{1}{2}$	$1\frac{1}{6}$	$1\frac{4}{9}$	$1\frac{2}{7}$
4.	$1\frac{1}{5}$	1	$1\frac{1}{7}$	$\frac{3}{5}$	$1\frac{1}{8}$
5.	$1\frac{1}{4}$	$1\frac{2}{5}$	$1\frac{3}{5}$	$1\frac{2}{7}$	$1\frac{3}{4}$

Lesson 4.2, page 38

	a	b	c	d	e
1.	$\frac{2}{3}$	$\frac{3}{4}$	$\frac{1}{2}$	$\frac{4}{9}$	$\frac{1}{2}$
2.	$\frac{1}{3}$	$\frac{1}{2}$	$\frac{1}{3}$	$\frac{1}{4}$	$\frac{2}{7}$
3.	$\frac{1}{5}$	$\frac{2}{5}$	$\frac{1}{2}$	$\frac{3}{8}$	$\frac{1}{3}$
4.	$\frac{1}{6}$	$\frac{1}{2}$	$\frac{1}{2}$	$\frac{2}{3}$	$\frac{1}{3}$
5.	$\frac{3}{5}$	$\frac{3}{8}$	$\frac{1}{3}$	$\frac{5}{6}$	$\frac{3}{7}$

Grade 6 Answers

Lesson 4.3, page 39

	a	b	c	d	e
1.	$1\frac{3}{8}$	$1\frac{13}{30}$	$1\frac{5}{12}$	$1\frac{1}{5}$	$1\frac{1}{24}$
2.	$\frac{1}{8}$	$\frac{1}{5}$	$\frac{3}{8}$	$\frac{5}{12}$	$\frac{2}{9}$
3.	$1\frac{1}{4}$	$1\frac{1}{8}$	$1\frac{4}{9}$	$\frac{19}{24}$	$1\frac{11}{30}$
4.	$\frac{1}{12}$	$\frac{1}{2}$	$\frac{3}{8}$	$\frac{7}{12}$	$\frac{1}{12}$

Lesson 4.4, page 40

	a	b	c	d
1.	$5\frac{7}{10}$	$8\frac{1}{8}$	$7\frac{1}{6}$	$6\frac{1}{3}$
2.	$3\frac{11}{12}$	$6\frac{1}{8}$	$4\frac{1}{2}$	$4\frac{7}{8}$
3.	$4\frac{7}{12}$	$8\frac{1}{8}$	$4\frac{5}{12}$	$7\frac{1}{8}$
4.	$7\frac{1}{3}$	$3\frac{5}{6}$	$8\frac{3}{8}$	$6\frac{23}{30}$

Lesson 4.5, page 41

	a	b	c	d
1.	$3\frac{5}{8}$	$4\frac{1}{2}$	$4\frac{3}{8}$	$4\frac{3}{10}$
2.	$1\frac{1}{8}$	$4\frac{1}{2}$	$2\frac{1}{12}$	$5\frac{3}{10}$
3.	$2\frac{1}{2}$	$\frac{1}{2}$	$4\frac{3}{5}$	$\frac{2}{3}$
4.	$1\frac{7}{8}$	$2\frac{5}{6}$	$2\frac{2}{5}$	$2\frac{1}{6}$

Lesson 4.6, page 42

1. $1\frac{5}{12}$; $\frac{1}{12}$ 2. $3\frac{1}{12}$ 3. $3\frac{7}{12}$ 4. $1\frac{2}{3}$ 5. $\frac{11}{12}$ 6. $3\frac{11}{15}$

Posttest, page 43

	a	b	c	d
1.	$2\frac{2}{3}$	$1\frac{1}{24}$	$\frac{7}{12}$	$1\frac{3}{20}$
2.	$\frac{3}{8}$	$\frac{5}{24}$	$\frac{3}{20}$	$\frac{19}{40}$
3.	$5\frac{17}{24}$	$4\frac{1}{12}$	$8\frac{7}{8}$	$8\frac{5}{21}$
4.	$4\frac{1}{12}$	$1\frac{1}{21}$	$2\frac{2}{3}$	$3\frac{3}{7}$
5.	$5\frac{11}{24}$	$8\frac{2}{3}$	$12\frac{5}{12}$	$5\frac{11}{15}$

Posttest, page 44

6. $\frac{17}{24}$; Jorge; $\frac{1}{24}$ 7. $4\frac{1}{6}$; $\frac{5}{6}$ 8. $9\frac{5}{12}$ 9. $3\frac{3}{4}$ 10. $18\frac{29}{40}$

Chapter 5

Pretest, page 45

	a	b	c
1.	$\frac{21}{32}$	$3\frac{3}{8}$	$3\frac{1}{8}$
2.	$12\frac{1}{2}$	$20\frac{4}{5}$	$40\frac{1}{2}$
3.	$13\frac{5}{12}$	$7\frac{1}{5}$	$4\frac{1}{8}$
4.	12	$\frac{4}{15}$	$26\frac{2}{3}$
5.	$\frac{32}{35}$	$\frac{4}{5}$	$\frac{3}{7}$
6.	$\frac{22}{25}$	$2\frac{2}{13}$	$\frac{59}{72}$

Pretest, page 46

7. $\frac{21}{32}$ 8. $3\frac{1}{8}$ 9. $4\frac{3}{8}$ 10. $13\frac{1}{8}$ 11. $16\frac{1}{2}$
12. $5\frac{1}{3}$ 13. $\frac{3}{4}$

Lesson 5.1, page 47

	a	b	c	d
1.	$\frac{4}{15}$	$\frac{5}{8}$	$\frac{5}{8}$	$\frac{3}{10}$
2.	$\frac{7}{16}$	$\frac{16}{27}$	$\frac{3}{10}$	$\frac{9}{35}$
3.	$\frac{1}{9}$	$\frac{11}{18}$	$\frac{4}{25}$	$\frac{9}{28}$
4.	$\frac{1}{12}$	$\frac{5}{48}$	$\frac{16}{27}$	$\frac{49}{64}$
5.	$\frac{35}{72}$	$\frac{9}{16}$	$\frac{9}{40}$	$\frac{6}{35}$
6.	$\frac{1}{7}$	$\frac{1}{8}$	$\frac{3}{5}$	$\frac{7}{36}$

Lesson 5.2, page 48

	a	b	c	d
1.	$1\frac{7}{8}$	$6\frac{2}{5}$	4	$3\frac{1}{2}$
2.	$3\frac{3}{5}$	$3\frac{3}{4}$	$1\frac{5}{7}$	$3\frac{3}{4}$
3.	4	$3\frac{3}{8}$	$1\frac{5}{7}$	$1\frac{1}{2}$
4.	$2\frac{2}{5}$	$4\frac{2}{3}$	$6\frac{3}{4}$	$2\frac{1}{2}$
5.	3	$\frac{7}{8}$	$1\frac{1}{3}$	$1\frac{7}{8}$

Lesson 5.3, page 49

	a	b	c	d
1.	$7\frac{1}{2}$	$6\frac{3}{4}$	28	14
2.	$23\frac{5}{8}$	$16\frac{1}{2}$	$9\frac{1}{3}$	$15\frac{5}{8}$
3.	$7\frac{1}{2}$	$24\frac{1}{2}$	$10\frac{5}{8}$	9
4.	$4\frac{6}{7}$	$36\frac{4}{5}$	7	$10\frac{3}{4}$
5.	$12\frac{1}{4}$	$9\frac{3}{4}$	$6\frac{3}{4}$	26

Lesson 5.4, page 50

	a	b	c	d
1.	$2\frac{5}{6}$	$4\frac{3}{8}$	$6\frac{33}{40}$	4
2.	$18\frac{2}{15}$	$20\frac{1}{4}$	$7\frac{7}{12}$	$8\frac{3}{4}$
3.	14	$5\frac{4}{9}$	$3\frac{21}{32}$	$3\frac{5}{6}$
4.	$5\frac{29}{32}$	$1\frac{4}{5}$	$2\frac{37}{48}$	15
5.	$4\frac{4}{5}$	$6\frac{1}{9}$	4	$4\frac{1}{3}$

Lesson 5.5, page 51

	a	b	c	d
1.	$\frac{8}{15}$	$\frac{15}{64}$	$\frac{8}{35}$	$\frac{1}{4}$
2.	$\frac{3}{14}$	$\frac{9}{16}$	$3\frac{1}{3}$	$2\frac{2}{3}$
3.	$\frac{7}{8}$	$1\frac{1}{2}$	$2\frac{2}{5}$	$3\frac{3}{4}$
4.	$8\frac{1}{4}$	$17\frac{1}{4}$	$26\frac{2}{3}$	14
5.	$13\frac{7}{8}$	$18\frac{1}{3}$	$2\frac{19}{40}$	$4\frac{3}{35}$
6.	$11\frac{2}{3}$	$4\frac{6}{7}$	$10\frac{5}{8}$	$3\frac{9}{16}$

Grade 6 Answers

Lesson 5.6, page 52
1. $\frac{1}{2}$ 2. $3\frac{1}{3}$ 3. $3\frac{3}{4}$ 4. $17\frac{1}{2}$ 5. 18 6. $8\frac{1}{3}$ 7. $20\frac{2}{5}$

Lesson 5.7, page 53
	a	b	c	d	e	f
1.	$\frac{3}{2}$	$\frac{8}{5}$	$\frac{4}{1}$	$\frac{8}{3}$	$\frac{6}{1}$	$\frac{7}{3}$
2.	$\frac{1}{2}$	$\frac{1}{3}$	$\frac{1}{5}$	$\frac{1}{9}$	$\frac{1}{8}$	$\frac{1}{5}$
3.	$\frac{1}{7}$	$\frac{3}{7}$	$\frac{3}{1}$	$\frac{2}{1}$	$\frac{4}{3}$	$\frac{5}{1}$
4.	$\frac{5}{4}$	$\frac{6}{5}$	$\frac{7}{1}$	$\frac{8}{11}$	$\frac{7}{6}$	$\frac{3}{10}$
5.	$\frac{9}{1}$	$\frac{4}{11}$	$\frac{9}{5}$	$\frac{9}{4}$	$\frac{2}{5}$	$\frac{1}{6}$
6.	$\frac{10}{7}$	$\frac{5}{2}$	$\frac{1}{1}$	$\frac{15}{1}$	$\frac{9}{7}$	$\frac{16}{7}$
7.	$\frac{9}{8}$	$\frac{1}{10}$	$\frac{7}{12}$	$\frac{16}{15}$	$\frac{2}{3}$	$\frac{3}{5}$
8.	$\frac{10}{9}$	$\frac{11}{8}$	$\frac{7}{2}$	$\frac{1}{4}$	$\frac{1}{15}$	$\frac{11}{12}$
9.	$\frac{1}{12}$	$\frac{13}{6}$	$\frac{3}{8}$	$\frac{15}{14}$	$\frac{13}{7}$	$\frac{1}{18}$
10.	$\frac{5}{3}$	$\frac{16}{9}$	$\frac{9}{5}$	$\frac{10}{3}$	$\frac{7}{4}$	$\frac{16}{7}$

Lesson 5.8, page 54
	a	b	c	d
1.	$7\frac{1}{2}$	$9\frac{3}{5}$	$2\frac{1}{2}$	$18\frac{2}{3}$
2.	12	12	25	$4\frac{4}{7}$
3.	$\frac{7}{40}$	$\frac{5}{48}$	$\frac{9}{40}$	$\frac{1}{15}$
4.	$\frac{4}{49}$	$\frac{5}{48}$	$\frac{1}{12}$	$\frac{1}{6}$

Lesson 5.9, page 55
	a	b	c	d
1.	$\frac{5}{6}$	$\frac{9}{16}$	$\frac{5}{6}$	$1\frac{1}{15}$
2.	$\frac{4}{7}$	$1\frac{1}{15}$	$2\frac{2}{9}$	$\frac{5}{6}$
3.	$2\frac{5}{8}$	$1\frac{1}{6}$	$\frac{1}{2}$	$2\frac{1}{2}$
4.	$\frac{9}{10}$	$1\frac{1}{27}$	$\frac{4}{5}$	$\frac{6}{7}$

Lesson 5.10, page 56
	a	b	c	d
1.	$\frac{3}{4}$	$\frac{1}{2}$	$2\frac{2}{7}$	$\frac{7}{15}$
2.	$3\frac{6}{7}$	$2\frac{1}{72}$	$\frac{13}{18}$	$\frac{12}{25}$
3.	$2\frac{2}{5}$	$\frac{1}{2}$	$1\frac{1}{3}$	$\frac{17}{24}$
4.	$\frac{9}{10}$	$1\frac{23}{57}$	$\frac{3}{13}$	$5\frac{2}{5}$

Lesson 5.11, page 57
	a	b	c	d
1.	$\frac{4}{3}$	$\frac{8}{11}$	$\frac{1}{3}$	$\frac{5}{2}$
2.	$5\frac{1}{3}$	10	$10\frac{1}{2}$	$3\frac{3}{7}$
3.	$1\frac{1}{2}$	$1\frac{1}{5}$	$\frac{9}{14}$	$\frac{24}{25}$
4.	$1\frac{3}{7}$	$\frac{6}{13}$	$2\frac{1}{4}$	2
5.	$1\frac{5}{12}$	$\frac{5}{8}$	$\frac{23}{30}$	$\frac{5}{8}$
6.	$\frac{21}{34}$	$1\frac{5}{21}$	$1\frac{11}{21}$	$\frac{3}{4}$

Lesson 5.12, page 58
1. $3\frac{1}{16}$ 2. 8 3. $\frac{7}{27}$ 4. $1\frac{1}{3}$ 5. 5 6. $2\frac{2}{5}$

Posttest, page 59
	a	b	c	d
1.	$\frac{1}{2}$	$\frac{3}{16}$	$\frac{21}{40}$	$\frac{5}{28}$
2.	$3\frac{1}{3}$	$3\frac{1}{2}$	$7\frac{1}{5}$	$4\frac{4}{7}$
3.	$12\frac{1}{2}$	$37\frac{1}{2}$	22	$16\frac{2}{3}$
4.	$8\frac{1}{3}$	$4\frac{1}{2}$	$6\frac{1}{4}$	$11\frac{4}{15}$
5.	$\frac{8}{3}$	$\frac{1}{5}$	$\frac{5}{12}$	$\frac{7}{4}$
6.	$7\frac{1}{2}$	$\frac{4}{25}$	$18\frac{2}{3}$	$\frac{7}{16}$
7.	$\frac{5}{6}$	$1\frac{5}{16}$	$1\frac{11}{21}$	$\frac{5}{9}$
8.	$1\frac{1}{4}$	$1\frac{1}{3}$	1	$\frac{12}{25}$

Posttest, page 60
9. $\frac{5}{18}$ 10. $3\frac{3}{4}$ 11. $8\frac{1}{3}$ 12. $11\frac{2}{3}$ 13. $10\frac{5}{6}$
14. $1\frac{1}{3}$ 15. $\frac{4}{5}$

Chapter 6

Pretest, page 61
	a	b	c	d	e
1.	0.2	0.23	0.4	0.75	0.98
2.	$\frac{3}{5}$	$\frac{2}{25}$	$2\frac{1}{4}$	$3\frac{3}{20}$	$2\frac{1}{5}$
3.	$<$	$=$	$>$		
4.	71.72	1034.12	74.835	106.918	
5.	39.727	3.57	5.775	52.079	
6.	$91.00	$4527.00	$79.97	$12.21	
7.	$46.33	$21.33	$0.49	$10.09	

Pretest, page 62
8. 2.5 in.; Monday; Wednesday; 1.4 in.; 0.2 in., 0.7 in., 1.6 in.
9. $41.45   10. $38.97   11. $50.15

Lesson 6.1, page 63
	a	b	c	d
1.	0.3	0.1	0.07	0.04
2.	2.4	7.6	21.02	58.09
3.	$\frac{2}{5}$	$\frac{4}{5}$	$\frac{3}{50}$	$\frac{39}{100}$
4.	$9\frac{3}{5}$	$13\frac{3}{10}$	$11\frac{4}{25}$	$685\frac{1}{20}$
5.	0.9	0.08		
6.	5.2	3.02		
7.	0.1	0.73		

8. two and seven tenths 9. sixty-two hundredths
10. five and eight hundredths

Grade 6 Answers

Lesson 6.2, page 64

	a	b	c
1.	0.007	0.025	0.561
2.	0.0004	0.0435	0.0508
3.	2.005	7.861	4.128
4.	5.0031	2.0165	8.0008
5.	$\frac{1}{500}$	$\frac{89}{1000}$	$\frac{41}{500}$
6.	$\frac{733}{1000}$	$\frac{33}{80}$	$\frac{63}{2000}$
7.	$3\frac{201}{10000}$	$6\frac{223}{1000}$	$4\frac{301}{1000}$
8.	$25\frac{1367}{10000}$	$3\frac{177}{1250}$	$7\frac{2003}{10000}$
9.	0.039	8.013	
10.	0.0049	2.0269	

Lesson 6.3, page 65

	a	b	c
1.	0.4	0.40	0.400
2.	3.5	0.12	0.680
3.	2.6	0.45	0.116
4.	2.2	0.34	1.270
5.	0.8	0.75	0.075
6.	7.5	2.30	0.056

Lesson 6.4, page 66

	a	b	c	d
1.	$\frac{2}{5}$	$\frac{3}{4}$	$3\frac{1}{10}$	$\frac{3}{5}$
2.	$\frac{1}{4}$	$1\frac{3}{10}$	$4\frac{3}{20}$	$2\frac{1}{5}$
3.	$3\frac{127}{1000}$	$\frac{4}{25}$	$8\frac{2}{5}$	$2\frac{1}{2}$
4.	$\frac{1}{1000}$	$\frac{1}{25}$	$1\frac{3}{5}$	$1\frac{1}{100}$
5.	$\frac{16}{25}$	$\frac{7}{10}$	$4\frac{3}{5}$	$\frac{22}{25}$
6.	$2\frac{21}{50}$	$\frac{14}{25}$	$\frac{3}{20}$	$\frac{1}{500}$
7.	$2\frac{3}{10}$	$3\frac{9}{10}$	$1\frac{19}{20}$	$\frac{221}{500}$
8.	$1\frac{43}{50}$	$3\frac{31}{100}$	$\frac{24}{25}$	$\frac{3}{25}$
9.	$4\frac{19}{25}$	$3\frac{89}{100}$	$4\frac{2}{25}$	$\frac{11}{20}$

Lesson 6.5, page 67

	a	b	c
1.	5.213 < 5.312	3.1 = 3.100	28.35 < 28.351
2.	6.32 > 6.032	5.17 < 5.172	144.3 > 144
3.	7.325 > 6.425	3.14 > 2.99	48.28 = 48.280
4.	0.2135 < 0.2233	1.006 < 1.060	0.010 > 0.001

5. 7.498, 7.52, 7.521, 7.6
6. 0.0088, 0.080, 0.082, 0.0823
7. 12.193, 12.1931, 12.2001, 12.201
8. 0.1084, 0.11639, 0.1164, 0.1171

Lesson 6.6, page 68

	a	b	c	d	e
1.	11.7	1.61	4.23	9.81	20.44
2.	2.315	40.21	44.339	10.52	6.35
3.	10.45	70.79	134.99	33.5	22.3
4.	8.1	77.16	46.344	101.1	4
5.	15.22	590.13	204.11	28.205	16.884
6.	0.771	12.596	94.211	8.142	102.5
7.	6.902	0.925	1.560	6.929	57.504

Lesson 6.7, page 69

	a	b	c	d	e
1.	0.5	0.8	1.9	0.69	1.5
2.	7.04	0.163	0.335	1.3	2.8
3.	16.3	0.37	0.33	2.567	7.11
4.	4.218	14.4	24.232	5.9	7.76
5.	16.8	9.145	26.16	41.7	95.3
6.	1.86	1.462	2.69	1.3	4.9
7.	69.2	36.458	5.54	3.7	6.17

Lesson 6.8, page 70

	a	b	c	d	e
1.	2.359	1.58	15.36	52.86	9.242
2.	0.47	1.26	2.361	0.814	4.65
3.	17.372	31.55	8.945	7.73	12.117
4.	6.09	8.84	11.04	5.535	18.783
5.	13.22	1.023	5.003	8.913	11.373
6.	57.96	0.64	94.857	2.79	8.03
7.	12.372	15.273	18.048	6.008	0.067

Lesson 6.9, page 71

	a	b	c	d	e
1.	$6.20	$4.43	$1.21	$684.09	$11.78
2.	$543.73	$133.66	$9927.93	$241.83	$123.38
3.	$103.81	$545.71	$8067.43	$456.11	$2.48
4.	$516.10	$1635.16	$7078.43	$74.58	$10.00
5.	$107.59	$95.80	$4211.30	$105.55	$16.72
6.	$7197.40	$2150.68	$98.90	$4.76	$2.57

Lesson 6.10, page 72

	a	b	c	d	e
1.	$87.37	$0.57	$6.28	$2.79	$7.08
2.	$231.19	$17.26	$5.26	$0.70	$5.96
3.	$187.69	$416.77	$326.45	$34.05	$55.56
4.	$274.70	$1778.87	$1.41	$557.05	$4641.43
5.	$44.97	$0.05	$0.81	$144.57	$45.34
6.	$34.17	$91.08	$5.91	$2.13	$726.82

Grade 6 Answers

	a	b	c	d	e
1.	0.4	0.037	0.2	0.25	0.46
2.	$\frac{4}{25}$	$\frac{19}{20}$	$2\frac{3}{4}$	$3\frac{1}{2}$	$4\frac{1}{100}$
3.	>	<	=		
4.	62.99	1132.55	80.742	115.558	
5.	42.368	3.93	4.838	25.088	
6.	$115.00	$3951.00	$29.48	$9.51	
7.	$35.23	$37.52	$0.45	$12.98	

Posttest, page 74

8. 18.9; 4.9; 5.7; 8.3; blue; white; 3.4
9. $26.45 **10.** $35.64 **11.** $46.25

Mid-Test

Page 75

	a	b	c	d	e
1.	1103	118602	3140	56213	20368
2.	2303	9215	24624	1802340	2562648
3.	12r8	7809	137r43	2581r10	428
4.	15.1	5.033	$87.70	$9.59	21.233
5.	900	500	5400	80	
6.	11000	4000	100000	700	

Page 76

7.	$2\frac{1}{3}$	$1\frac{3}{5}$	$1\frac{3}{7}$	$3\frac{5}{6}$	
8.	$\frac{25}{8}$	$\frac{27}{5}$	$\frac{32}{3}$	$\frac{27}{4}$	
9.	$2 \times 2 \times 2 \times 5$	$2 \times 3 \times 3 \times 3$	$2 \times 2 \times 3 \times 3$		
10.	$\frac{1}{2}$	$\frac{35}{48}$	$3\frac{3}{4}$	$9\frac{1}{3}$	14
11.	30	45	56		

Page 77

12.	1	$1\frac{5}{12}$	$1\frac{5}{24}$	$7\frac{11}{12}$	$4\frac{1}{2}$
13.	$\frac{1}{4}$	$\frac{1}{6}$	$5\frac{2}{5}$	$3\frac{1}{12}$	$2\frac{2}{3}$
14.	30	$\frac{3}{20}$	$1\frac{5}{16}$	$\frac{13}{15}$	$1\frac{7}{8}$
15.	2.5	2.50	2.500		
16.	$\frac{19}{50}$	$\frac{2}{25}$	$\frac{3}{250}$		
17.	$2\frac{7}{50}$	$3\frac{9}{10}$	$154\frac{83}{1000}$		

Page 78

18. 2506 **19.** 14.25 **20.** $\frac{7}{20}$ **21.** $3\frac{1}{24}$
22. $67.38 **23.** 1,157

Chapter 7

Pretest, page 79

	a	b	c	d
1.	0.858	857.52	40.976	0.3526
2.	$1,128.32	$1256.48	65.2	0.037
3.	27.9912	3.21126	0.001344	2.4618

4.	5.7	12.33	800	2420
5.	0.06	750	2.65	0.005
6.	$.55	$5.68	175	0.025

Pretest, page 80

7. 16.8 lb. **8.** 21 ft. **9.** 2.964 lb. **10.** $2.63
11. 23 **12.** 140

Lesson 7.1, page 81

	a	b	c	d	e
1.	5.6	0.04	0.0975	13.44	17.5
2.	0.0918	0.0486	28.105	2.1087	275.04
3.	19.8468	206.703	303.986	20.4102	563.85
4.	95.934	58.734	15.036	2.2382	0.6724
5.	0.1698	9.434	0.1909	0.09	12.532

Lesson 7.2, page 82

	a	b	c	d
1.	$5.74	$1.53	$10.56	$29.26
2.	$691.74	$2436.84	$513.75	$263.14
3.	$538.23	$436.05	$1135.55	$2227.53
4.	$1404.00	$5146.20	$4397.58	$6007.44
5.	$1507.22	$11448.80	$903.90	$3255.63

Lesson 7.3, page 83

	a	b	c	d	e
1.	65.42	42.5	26.45	5264	6.32
2.	1064	1064	64010	0.3	0.62
3.	0.25	632	2593	932.5	7245
4.	3200	0.023	27620	18.3	318
5.	21.13	121.3	3.211	233.9	3239

Lesson 7.3, page 84

	a	b	c	d
1.	53.636	0.1825	0.000128	14.665
2.	42.599	284.928	49.174	13.6272
3.	34.2633	104.346	32.2125	0.3286
4.	$282.92	$593.94	$16.72	$653.48
5.	27.5422	0.0009	0.0021	2.0894
6.	26.753	17609.4	0.1035	121.572

Lesson 7.4, page 85

1. 20.8 lb. **2.** 23.125 in. **3.** $370 **4.** $54.48
5. 0.465 lb. **6.** 0.351 in.

Lesson 7.5, page 86

	a	b	c	d
1.	7.7	0.49	0.205	0.173
2.	0.909	0.411	5.008	0.294
3.	0.62	0.0058	2.47	5.65
4.	1.87	0.0375	0.78	6.2

Grade 6 Answers

Lesson 7.6, page 87

	a	b	c	d
1.	60	200	360	42
2.	400	2250	300	500
3.	9000	2000	9000	94000
4.	4690	45400	3000	990

Lesson 7.7, page 88

	a	b	c	d
1.	0.21	56	3	51
2.	36	3.5	4200	24.58
3.	0.009	452	500	1.6
4.	22500	720	0.032	48

Lesson 7.8, page 89

	a	b	c	d
1.	2.2	85	0.4	1.5
2.	40	5.3	40	65
3.	3000	30	0.25	1.2
4.	0.04	40	5	6

Lesson 7.9, page 90

	a	b	c	d
1.	$8.45	$52.23	$52.76	$45
2.	$5.88	$8.55	$0.03	$.23
3.	$3.86	$40	$0.25	$8
4.	$25	$2	$3.50	$.05
5.	$501.20	$15	$2.25	$.02

Lesson 7.10, page 91

	a	b	c
1.	$54.20	$8.75	$12.50
2.	80	520	14000
3.	0.14	31	13
4.	5.8	140	0.025

Lesson 7.11, page 92

1. 40 mi.   2. 60   3. 15   4. 25   5. 372   6. 300

Posttest, page 93

	a	b	c	d
1.	3.512	1899.56	35.76	0.4028
2.	$1206.66	$1551.35	3.12	0.26
3.	32.4612	5.99122	0.001596	3.7109
4.	6.7	11.33	130	8200
5.	0.12	720	3.24	0.005
6.	$0.75	$5.62	50	0.035

Posttest, page 94

7. 24.75 lb.   8. 35.2 ft.   9. 5.208 lb.
10. $1.88   11. 32   12. 130

Chapter 8

Pretest, page 95

	a	b	c
1.	6%	30%	40%
2.	55%	28%	26%
3.	8%	70%	32%
4.	18.2%	225%	75%
5.	0.12	0.65	0.36
6.	0.0575	1.5	0.001
7.	$\frac{7}{20}$	$\frac{13}{25}$	$\frac{4}{25}$
8.	$\frac{3}{4}$	$\frac{4}{5}$	$\frac{11}{20}$
9.	1.2	8.74	10.5
10.	5.76	14.62	22
11.	3.54	10.5	24
12.	0.8	2.24	66.64

Pretest, page 96

13. 75%   14. 85%   15. 46   16. $11.98
17. 16.25 lb.   18. 1,170

Lesson 8.1, page 97

	Fraction	Decimal
1.	$\frac{1}{50}$	0.02
2.	$\frac{2}{25}$	0.08
3.	$\frac{27}{100}$	0.27
4.	$\frac{13}{100}$	0.13
5.	$\frac{17}{25}$	0.68
6.	$\frac{18}{25}$	0.72
7.	$\frac{14}{25}$	0.56
8.	$\frac{11}{100}$	0.11
9.	$\frac{3}{100}$	0.03
10.	$\frac{11}{50}$	0.22
11.	$\frac{17}{100}$	0.17
12.	$\frac{83}{100}$	0.23
13.	$\frac{97}{100}$	0.97
14.	$\frac{43}{100}$	0.43

Lesson 8.2, page 98

	a	b	c	d
1.	$\frac{3}{10}$	45%	$\frac{19}{100}$	26%
2.	75%	$\frac{8}{25}$	80%	$\frac{12}{25}$
3.	150%	$\frac{11}{25}$	65%	$\frac{14}{25}$
4.	$1\frac{1}{10}$	175%	$\frac{17}{25}$	95%
5.	60%	$\frac{1}{20}$	52%	$\frac{37}{50}$
6.	$\frac{57}{100}$	14%	$\frac{3}{25}$	76%

7.	$\frac{3}{50}$	70%	$\frac{19}{50}$	108%
8.	90%	$\frac{18}{25}$	54%	$1\frac{3}{5}$
9.	$\frac{17}{20}$	10%	$\frac{73}{100}$	$\frac{39}{100}$
10.	20%	$\frac{21}{25}$	115%	35%
11.	$\frac{7}{20}$	30%	$\frac{29}{50}$	$\frac{1}{25}$
12.	125%	$1\frac{2}{5}$	130%	28%

Lesson 8.3, page 99

	a	b	c
1.	0.04	350%	0.165
2.	51%	0.006	34.5%
3.	0.33	2.5%	0.15
4.	8%	1.25	63%
5.	75%	0.88	47.8%
6.	0.98	12.5%	0.045
7.	70%	0.21	23%
8.	0.035	45%	0.735
9.	29%	30%	0.01
10.	1.01	2	6%
11.	62.5%	0.64	0.0115
12.	0.57	85%	42.5%

Lesson 8.4, page 100

	a	b
1.	$5\frac{1}{5}$	76
2.	$9\frac{3}{5}$	7
3.	18	$7\frac{1}{2}$
4.	$1\frac{24}{25}$	$3\frac{4}{5}$
5.	8	$6\frac{3}{4}$
6.	64	15
7.	$31\frac{1}{2}$	$8\frac{1}{10}$
8.	$3\frac{17}{25}$	$14\frac{2}{5}$
9.	54	$21\frac{1}{2}$
10.	$4\frac{4}{5}$	$5\frac{2}{5}$
11.	36	19
12.	$10\frac{1}{2}$	$\frac{3}{4}$

Lesson 8.5, page 101

	a	b
1.	20.48	10.4
2.	2.225	4.62
3.	6.96	20
4.	6.132	42.14
5.	2.048	3.19
6.	42	4.5
7.	5.88	38

8.	9	31.24
9.	5.796	64
10.	7.84	27.9
11.	2.56	24
12.	4.32	2.7

Lesson 8.6, page 102
1. $48.65 2. $194.60 3. 18 4. 480 5. $90
6. 375

Posttest, page 103

	a	b	c
1.	13%	70%	80%
2.	45%	44%	78%
3.	2%	90%	23%
4.	182%	2.25%	25%
5.	0.23	0.85	1.75
6.	0.0125	0.03	0.006
7.	$\frac{11}{20}$	$\frac{14}{25}$	$\frac{6}{25}$
8.	$\frac{3}{5}$	$\frac{1}{4}$	$\frac{17}{20}$
9.	1.4	9.24	21.84
10.	4.92	13.92	39
11.	5.52	16.5	36
12.	1.8	3.51	84.48

Posttest, page 104
13. 60% 14. $\frac{11}{20}$ 15. $4,375 16. 42 17. 4.4 lb.
18. 847

Chapter 9

Pretest, page 105

	a	b
1.	96 in.	9 ft.
2.	20 yd.	15,840 ft.
3.	33 ft.	14 ft.
4.	91 in.	151 in.
5.	33 qt.	52 pt.
6.	83 pt.	23 qt.
7.	11 pt.	$2\frac{1}{4}$ gal.
8.	26 gal.	266 pt.
9.	400 oz.	960 oz.
10.	46,000 lb.	140 oz.
11.	304 oz.	$\frac{3}{4}$ lb.
12.	17 lb.	29 T.

Pretest, page 106
13. 75 ft.; 70 yd. 14. 240 sq. in.; $187\frac{1}{2}$ sq. ft.
15. 960 cu. ft.; 2,880 cu. in. 16. 165 sq. ft.
17. 300 cu. in. 18. 54 ft.

Grade 6 Answers

Lesson 9.1, page 107

	a	b	c
1.	84 in.	6 ft.	45 ft.
2.	3 yd.	21,120 ft.	7,040 yd.
3.	9 ft.	10 ft.	14 yd.
4.	55 in.	81 in.	$2\frac{1}{2}$ ft.
5.	3 mi.	18 ft.	216 in.
6.	23 ft.	276 in.	8 yd.
7.	141 in.	11,060 ft.	10 yd.
8.	300 in.	12 ft.	4 yd.
9.	8,800 yd.	$1\frac{1}{2}$ ft.	36 ft.
10.	432 in.	$\frac{1}{2}$ mi.	188 in.
11.	662 in.	5,280 yd.	$\frac{1}{2}$ ft.
12.	14 ft.	27 yd.	14 yd.

Lesson 9.2, page 108

	a	b	c
1.	14 c.	36 pt.	60 qt.
2.	27 gal.	2 pt.	8 pt.
3.	$1\frac{1}{2}$ qt.	30 gal.	84 c.
4.	19 qt.	19 c.	$7\frac{1}{2}$ gal.
5.	20 qt.	12 pt.	3 pt.
6.	15 pt.	29 qt.	96 qt.
7.	23 pt.	$\frac{1}{2}$ gal.	26 qt.
8.	13 gal.	288 pt.	36 gal.
9.	20 qt.	40 pt.	40 pt.
10.	80 pt.	160 gal.	11 c.
11.	4 pt.	8 c.	8 c.
12.	$\frac{1}{2}$ gal.	$\frac{1}{2}$ gal.	16 c.

Lesson 9.3, page 109

	a	b
1.	1,040 oz.	6 lb.
2.	8 lb.	800 oz.
3.	2 lb.	64 oz.
4.	10,000 lb.	113 oz.
5.	640 oz.	$12\frac{1}{2}$ T.
6.	$\frac{3}{4}$ lb.	14,400 lb.
7.	184 oz.	$\frac{1}{2}$ lb.
8.	$3\frac{1}{4}$ lb.	9 lb.
9.	80 oz.	320 oz.
10.	20,000 lb.	158 oz.
11.	32 oz.	$\frac{1}{4}$ lb.
12.	11 lb.	9 T.

Lesson 9.4, page 110

1. 59 in.; 36 ft. **2.** 86 yd.; 26 ft.
3. 40 sq. in.; $27\frac{1}{2}$ sq. ft. **4.** $12\frac{1}{2}$ sq. ft.; 36 sq. yd.

Lesson 9.5, page 111

	a	b	c
1.	420 cu. yd.	512 cu. in.	12,000 cu. ft.
2.	336 cu. ft.	100 cu. in.	648 cu. in.
3.	250 cu. ft.	300 cu. in.	10,800 cu. in.

Lesson 9.6, page 112

1. 156 ft. **2.** 1,440 cu. in.
3. 480 sq. yd.; 120 yd. **4.** 36 cu. in.
5. 375 sq. in. **6.** 360 ft.

Posttest, page 113

	a	b
1.	108 in.	7 ft.
2.	5 yd.	31,680 ft.
3.	27 ft.	15 ft.
4.	79 in.	369 in.
5.	25 qt.	32 pt.
6.	43 pt.	13 qt.
7.	3 pt.	$1\frac{1}{2}$ gal.
8.	23 gal.	344 pt.
9.	240 oz.	480 oz.
10.	40,000 lb.	108 oz.
11.	192 oz.	$\frac{1}{2}$ lb.
12.	13 lb.	14 T.

Posttest, page 114

13. 89 ft.; 139 ft. **14.** 315 sq. in.; $76\frac{1}{2}$ sq. ft.
15. 980 cu. yd.; 11,200 cu. ft. **16.** 216 sq. ft.
17. 2,400 cu. in. **18.** 5,040 cu. in.; 420 cu. ft.

Chapter 10

Pretest, page 115

	a	b	c
1.	580 mm	5.8 cm	0.58 m
2.	2,600 m	0.0062 km	0.05 m
3.	7.25 m	6,380 mm	460 mm
4.	5,000 mL	0.007 kL	0.35 L
5.	0.005 L	600 L	81 mL
6.	0.0038 L	0.0054 kL	1,400 mL
7.	9.5 kg	0.04 kg	0.007 kg
8.	4,000 g	380 g	0.053 g
9.	420 mg	0.057 g	6,200 mg

Grade 6 Answers

Pretest, page 116

10. 67 cm; 180 mm; 107 m
11. 69.36 sq. cm; 1,024 sq. m; 6,696 sq. mm
12. 1,200 cu. cm; 2,700 cu. mm; 384 cu. mm
13. 50   **14.** 2.4 kg

Lesson 10.1, page 117

	a	b	c
1.	4.6 cm	0.046 m	0.35 km
2.	230 cm	3,200 mm	0.0032 km
3.	0.52 cm	0.0076 m	67 mm
4.	3,000 m	4.2 cm	0.042 km
5.	6 cm	0.0385 km	3,850 cm
6.	0.013 m	8 mm	0.008 m
7.	0.342 km	40 cm	0.5 km
8.	64.5 cm	580 mm	8.73 km
9.	5,830 mm	32,000 m	5,000 m
10.	3 mm	30 mm	45,000 mm

Lesson 10.2, page 118

	a	b	c
1.	2,000 mL	0.002 kL	2,000 L
2.	0.033 L	4,220 L	0.04 L
3.	2730 L	0.273 L	40,000 mL
4.	0.8 L	0.45 kL	0.012 L
5.	0.0052 L	0.0052 kL	3.76 L
6.	7.6 kL	3.5 L	5,000 mL
7.	50 mL		
8.	600		
9.	1,890 mL		

Lesson 10.3, page 119

	a	b	c
1.	4,000 g	0.004 kg	4,000 mg
2.	0.073 g	3,660 g	0.03 g
3.	2,600 g	0.265 kg	40,000 mg
4.	0.9 kg	720 mg	0.0008 kg
5.	0.492 kg	0.006 kg	6,000 mg
6.	86.4 kg	1,200 g	0.004 g
7.	1.6 kg		
8.	440 kg		
9.	11.39 kg		

Lesson 10.4, page 120

	a	b
1.	19.4 cm	41 m
2.	240 mm	28 cm
3.	450 sq. cm	100 sq. m
4.	70 sq. mm	576 sq. cm

Lesson 10.5, page 121

	a	b	c
1.	576 cu. cm	1,728 cu. cm	2,112 cu. m
2.	1,44 cu. mm	1,620 cu. mm	3,600 cu. cm
3.	1,280 cu. mm	12,000 cu. cm	7,800 cu. mm

Lesson 10.6, page 122

1. 90 m **2.** 0.102 cu. m **3.** 1,260 sq. cm
4. 87.72 sq. m **5.** 3,000 cu. cm **6.** 52 cm

Lesson 10.7, page 123

	a	b	c
1.	4.54 kg	992,250 mg	141.75 g
2.	0.56 kg	7.72 kg	1.26 kg
3.	9,922,500 mg	0.2 kg	45.4 kg
4.	70 kg	2,835 g	198,450 mg
5.	254 mm	21.96 m	49.88 km
6.	93.98 cm	39.30 m	40.26 m

Lesson 10.8, page 124

	a	b	c
1.	14.48 km	139.7 cm	2,082.8 mm
2.	30.5 m	19.19 m	25,400 mm
3.	2.37 L	11.35 L	26.50 L
4.	33.11 L	2,649.5 L	1.89 L
5.	300 mL	8.30 L	10.41 L
6.	367.15 L	1,620 mL	17.86 L
7.	2 in. > 5 cm	1 ft. < 60 cm	1 yd. < 2.7 m
8.	56 oz. > 75 g	4 qt. < 5 L	10 gal. < 38 L
9.	8 c. < 2 L	15 lb. > 5 kg	12 mi. > 12 km
10.	22 oz. > 20 mL	10 oz. > 280 g	15 yd. > 13.5 m

Posttest, page 125

	a	b	c
1.	650 mm	6.5 cm	0.65 m
2.	5800 m	0.0072 km	0.07 m
3.	8.67 m	3,680 mm	920 mm
4.	8,000 mL	0.003 kL	0.53 L
5.	0.008 L	900 L	34 mL
6.	0.0022 L	0.0037 kL	6,100 mL
7.	8.7 kg	0.08 kg	0.005 kg
8.	2,000 g	270 g	0.077 g
9.	380 mg	0.063 g	5,700 mg

Posttest, page 126

10. 80 m; 140 cm; 215 mm
11. 392 sq. cm; 3.61 sq. m; 5,406 sq. mm
12. 3,360 cubic m; 192 cubic mm; 1,200 cubic cm
13. 30
14. 3.2

Grade 6 Answers

Chapter 11

Pretest, page 127

1. 10 mi. 2. 5 3. Angelica 4. 5 mi.
5.

Stem	Leaves
1	8
2	4 5
3	1 6
5	6
7	2

6. mean 80; median 82; mode 66; range 32
7. $\frac{1}{5}$; $\frac{8}{15}$
   $\frac{1}{3}$; $\frac{4}{5}$

Pretest, page 128

8. sports 9. band 10. chorus 11. band
12.

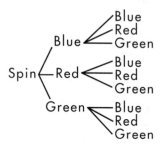

13. mean 12; median 12; mode 12; range 14
14. $\frac{1}{5}$; $\frac{2}{5}$
    $\frac{3}{5}$; $\frac{4}{5}$

Lesson 11.1, page 129

1. chorus 2. sports 3. newspaper 4. 2
5. 7 6. 3 7. 10 8. newspaper 9. 11
10. newspaper

Lesson 11.2, page 130

1. Lopez 2. 30 3. Wed. 4. Martin
5. 55 6. Wed. 7. Thurs. 8. Tues. 9. 105
10. 195

Lesson 11.3, page 131

1. carnations 2. 10 3. 5 4. 20 5. 5
6. $300 7. $90 8. $75 9. $300
10. $765

Lesson 11.4, page 132

	a	b
1.	$35\frac{3}{5}$	14
	35	12
	43	12
	18	15
2.	13	$20\frac{1}{6}$
	12	$18\frac{1}{2}$
	12	15
	8	13
3.	68	51
	71	49
	79	37
	27	49

Lesson 11.5, page 133

1.

a

Stem	Leaves
1	3 4
2	1 8
3	1 3 4

Key: 1 | 3 = 13

b

Stem	Leaves
3	8 9
4	9
5	0 4 7
6	3 4
7	2 9

Key: 3 | 8 = 38

Stem	Leaves
2	5 7
3	4 7 8
4	8 9

Key: 2 | 5 = 25

Stem	Leaves
7	3 5
8	1 4 7 8
9	1 3 6 9

Key: 7 | 3 = 73

Stem	Leaves
1	3 7 9
2	4 5
3	3 8

Key: 1 | 3 = 13

Stem	Leaves
2	3 5 6 7
3	3 5 7
4	1 5 6

Key: 2 | 3 = 23

Lesson 11.6, page 134

1. 75 **2.** 9 **3.** 50 **4.** 20 **5.** 15 **6.** 30

7.
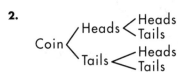

Lesson 11.7, page 135

1.
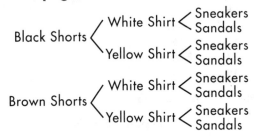

2.
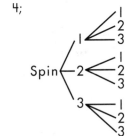

3. 4;

$$\text{Spin} \begin{cases} 1 \begin{cases} 1 \\ 2 \\ 3 \end{cases} \\ 2 \begin{cases} 1 \\ 2 \\ 3 \end{cases} \\ 3 \begin{cases} 1 \\ 2 \\ 3 \end{cases} \end{cases}$$

Lesson 11.8, page 136

1. $\frac{3}{10}$; $\frac{4}{5}$; $\frac{7}{10}$ **2.** $\frac{1}{6}$ **3.** $\frac{1}{2}$ **4.** $\frac{1}{3}$ **5.** $\frac{1}{3}$

6. $\frac{5}{6}$ **7.** $\frac{2}{3}$

Posttest, page 137

1. $20 **2.** 2 **3.** Lucas **4.** $260

5.
Stem	Leaves
1	2 8
2	2 2 5
3	1 6 8

Key: 1 | 2 = 12

6. mean 44; median 45; mode 47; range 21

7. $\frac{5}{12}$; $\frac{2}{3}$

$\frac{1}{4}$; $\frac{7}{12}$

Posttest, page 138

8. basketball **9.** volleyball **10.** soccer and football

11. volleyball

12. 2;
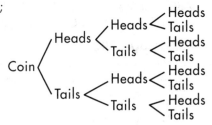

13. mean 13; median 13; mode 13; range 14

14. $\frac{1}{8}$; $\frac{3}{8}$

$\frac{1}{2}$; $\frac{1}{2}$

Chapter 12

Pretest, page 139

1. B **2.** G **3.** J **4.** PQR or RQP, obtuse, 130°;
   DEF or FED, acute, 54°; RST or TSR, right, 90°

5. V **6.** S **7.** V **8.** S **9.** C **10.** A; R; O; R

Pretest, page 140

11. X **12.** X **13.** $\overline{XW}$, $\overline{XY}$, $\overline{XZ}$ **14.** $\overline{RT}$ or $\overline{YZ}$

15. $\overline{YZ}$ or $\overline{ZY}$ **16.** C; N **17.** G **18.** E

19. D **20.** F **21.** A **22.** B **23.** D

24. H **25.** D, J **26.** K

Lesson 12.1, page 141

	a		b	
1.	A ● B	$\overleftrightarrow{AB}$	C ● D	$\overline{CD}$
2.	F ● G	$\overrightarrow{FG}$	F ● G	$\overrightarrow{GF}$
3.	H ● K	$\overline{HK}$	H ● K	$\overleftrightarrow{HK}$
4.	H ● K	$\overrightarrow{KH}$	H ● K	$\overrightarrow{HK}$
5.	C ● D	$\overleftrightarrow{CD}$	C ● D	$\overline{DC}$
6.	Ray	$\overrightarrow{PQ}$	Line Segment	$\overline{PQ}$
7.	Ray	$\overrightarrow{SR}$	Line	$\overleftrightarrow{RS}$
8.	Point	T	Ray	$\overrightarrow{MN}$
9.	Line Segment	$\overline{KL}$	Line	$\overleftrightarrow{KL}$
10.	Ray	$\overrightarrow{AB}$	Ray	$\overrightarrow{BA}$

Grade 6 Answers

Lesson 12.2, page 142
1. LJK or KJL; R; 90   2. MNO or ONM; A; 45
3. RST or TSR; O; 130   4. DEF or FED; R; 90
5. ABC or CBA; A; 40   6. PQR or RQP; O; 110
7. RST or TSR; R; 90   8. GHK or KHG; A; 35

Lesson 12.3, page 143
1. vertical   2. supplementary   3. supplementary
4. vertical   5. vertical   6. supplementary
7. 72°   8. 68°   9. 37°   10. 60°

Lesson 12.4, page 144

	a	b	c
1.	right	acute	obtuse
2.	obtuse	right	acute
3.	acute	obtuse	right
4.	right	obtuse	acute

Lesson 12.5, page 145
1. A, B, F, G, L   2. B, C, F, G, M   3. D, K
4. B, F, G   5. E, H   6. B, F, G   7. A, B, F, G, K, L
8. C, D, E, H, M, K   9. K   10. A, B, F, G, K, L
11. C, D, E, H, M   12. no

Lesson 12.6, page 146

	a	b
1.	N	C
2.	C	C
3.	C	C
4.	$\overline{AB} = 2$ cm	$\angle A = 58°$
5.	$\overline{BC} = 2.5$ cm	$\angle B = 80°$
6.	$\overline{AC} = 3$ cm	$\angle C = 42°$
7.	$\angle D = 36°$	$\overline{DE} = 5.4$ cm
8.	$\angle E = 52°$	$\overline{EF} = 3.1$ cm
9.	$\angle F = 92°$	$\overline{DF} = 4.3$ cm
10.	yes, triangles are congruent	

Lesson 12.7, page 147
1. diameter; chord; radius; chord
2. O   3. O
4. $\overline{OT}$, $\overline{OS}$, $\overline{OR}$
5. $\overline{MN}$, $\overline{TR}$ 6. $\overline{TR}$
7. Answers will vary. One possible answer is shown.

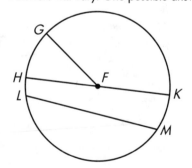

Lesson 12.8, page 148
1. triangular pyramid
2. rectangular solid
3. cylinder
4. triangular solid
5. square pyramid
6. cone
7. 4; 6; 4
8. 6; 12; 8
9. 0 vertices
10. 5; 9; 6
11. 5; 8; 5
12. 1 vertex

Posttest, page 149
1. ray, $\overrightarrow{AB}$; segment, $\overline{RS}$ or $\overline{SR}$
2. line, $\overleftrightarrow{CD}$ or $\overleftrightarrow{DC}$; line, $\overleftrightarrow{JK}$ or $\overleftrightarrow{KJ}$
3. ray, $\overrightarrow{FE}$; segment, $\overline{LM}$ or $\overline{ML}$
4. PQR or RQP, A, 52°; L MN or NML, R, 90°; ABC or CBA, O, 120°
5. 130°   6. 50°   7. 130°   8. 25°   9. A; R; O

Posttest, page 150
10. S   11. S   12. $\overline{ST}$, $\overline{SR}$, $\overline{SV}$ or $\overline{TS}$, $\overline{RS}$, $\overline{VS}$
13. $\overline{RV}$ or $\overline{VR}$ 14. $\overline{WV}$ or $\overline{VW}$ 15. C; C   16. H
17. K   18. E   19. J   20. D   21. G   22. A
23. B   24. C   25. F

Chapter 13

Pretest, page 151
1. 20; 13; 8   2. 8; 2; 15
3. Commutative; Associative; Property of Zero
4. Identity; Commutative; Identity
5. $(4 \times 6) + (4 \times 2)$; $2 \times (5 + 4)$; $(4 \times 2) + (4 \times 6)$
6. 18; 14; 20   7. expression; equation; expression
8. 5, y; 2, x; n; 1   9. 3; −7; 8
10. $2 < 7$; $−1 > −4$; $5 > 0$ 11. −3; −7; 0

Pretest, page 152

	a	b	c
12.	8	2	2
13.	11	0	0
14.	7	16	10
15.	16	1	25
16.	$1\frac{1}{2}$	36	3
17.	100	5	9
18.	$2 \times 2 \times 2 \times 2$	9×9	$5 \times 5 \times 5$
19.	4^4	2^3	6^5
20.	81	125	1

	a	b
21.	D	(4, 7)
22.	E	(7, 5)
23.	B	(5, 6)
24.	A	(7, 1)
25.	C	(3, 2)

Lesson 13.1, page 153

	a	b	c
1.	multiply	multiply	add
2.	subtract	divide	divide
3.	add	subtract	add
4.	10	23	
5.	8	8	
6.	9	1	
7.	8	20	
8.	10	2	
9.	8	8	
10.	40	40	
11.	1	5	
12.	32	32	

Lesson 13.2, page 154

	a	b
1.	Commutative	Associative
2.	Identity	Commutative
3.	Associative	Property of Zero
4.	Identity	Commutative
5.	$3 + (5 + 2)$	7×5
6.	4	$(3 \times 2) \times 5$
7.	$9 + 7$	$2 + (5 + 4)$
8.	7	37
9.	0	0

Lesson 13.3, page 155

	a	b
1.	multiply	add
2.	add	multiply
3.	$(4 \times 6) + (4 \times 2)$	$2 \times (5 + 4)$
4.	$5 \times (1 + 6)$	$(4 \times 2) + (4 \times 6)$
5.	$(8 \times 4) + (8 \times 3)$	$5 \times (0 + 1)$
6.	5	2
7.	6	5
8.	2	4
9.	16	16
10.	21	25

Lesson 13.4, page 156

	a	b	c
1.	expression	equation	expression
2.	equation	expression	equation
3.	$3; x$	$4; y$	
4.	$1; z$	$5; n$	
5.	$7; b$	$1; m$	
6.	$1; r$	$6; d$	
7.	$n + 5$	$8 - x$	
8.	$x + 7$	$n \times 11$	
9.	$6n = 18$	$70 - n = 29$	
10.	$\frac{8}{n} = 2$	$7 \times 12 = 84$	

11. Six decreased by a number is equal to three.
12. The product of five and thirteen is equal to sixty-five.

Lesson 13.5, page 157

	a	b	c
1.	addition	subtraction	
2.	subtraction	addition	
3.	6	4	17
4.	11	12	0
5.	12	10	0
6.	3	21	9
7.	0	20	4
8.	30	15	10
9.	$x + \$6 = \$20; x = \$14$		
10.	$g + 12 = 27; g = 15$		

Lesson 13.6, page 158

	a	b	c
1.	divide	multiply	
2.	multiply	divide	
3.	3	25	12
4.	9	1	8
5.	2	16	5
6.	3	$2\frac{1}{2}$	10
7.	$\frac{1}{4}$	20	81
8.	2	40	3
9.	36	6	10
10.	40	16	1
11.	6	150	3
12.	4	4	8

Lesson 13.7, page 159

	a	b	c
1.	3×10^1	4×10^3	5×10^4
2.	6×10^5	7×10^2	9×10^1
3.	4×10^4	1×10^5	4×10^2
4.	3 x 3 x 3	5 x 5 x 5 x 5	1 x 1 x 1 x 1 x 1 x 1
5.	12 x 12	8 x 8 x 8	6 x 6 x 6
6.	7 x 7 x 7 x 7	4 x 4 x 4 x 4	11 x 11 x 11 x 11

Grade 6 Answers

7.	3^3	8^2	7^5
8.	24^2	4^3	6^6
9.	2^4	38^3	5^5
10.	16	64	1
11.	64	81	125
12.	243	216	121

Lesson 13.8, page 160

	a	b	c
1.	−2	−7	1
2.	6	3	−5
3.	2<7	−1 > −4	5 > 0
4.	−4<1	0 > −8	−8 > −10
5.	7 > −7	−2 < 0	4 < 6
6.	1 > −1	6 > 3	−6 < −3
7.	4 > −2	−6 < −4	3 > −3
8.	−5, −3, 0	−8, 2, 8	
9.	−7, −3, 0, 5	−2, −1, 2, 4	
10a.	−6, −3, −2, 2, 5	**10b.** −8, −3, −2, 0, 5	

Lesson 13.9, page 161

	a	b	c	d
1.	7	−7	−1	1
2.	−6	0	0	6
3.	4	−4	−6	6
4.	−4	−10	4	10
5.	11	−3	3	−11
6.	0	−16	16	0
7.	−3	3	−11	1
8.	−1	11	−8	8
9.	3	−9	9	−3
10.	−10	−2	2	10

Lesson 13.10, page 162

1. J; E **2.** H; G **3.** L; M **4.** C; K **5.** F; D
6. (1, 6); (8, 8) **7.** (8, 3); (6, 5) **8.** (7, 1); (5, 7)
9. (1, 4); (2, 2) **10.** (4, 8); (4, 1)
11.

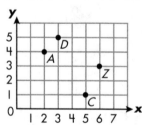

Posttest, page 163

1. 8; 6; 0 **2.** 8; 13; 10
3. Commutative; Associative; Property of Zero
4. Identity; Commutative; Identity
5. $(3 \times 5) + (3 \times 1)$; $4 \times (6 + 5)$; $(7 \times 3) + (7 \times 6)$
6. 28; 30; 18
7. expression; equation; expression
8. 9, y; 4, b; 1, m
9. −5; 8; −1 **10.** 3<9; −9 < −4; −5 < 0
11. −3; −8; 0

Posttest, page 164

	a	b	c
12.	8	3	4
13.	27	16	0
14.	7	0	6
15.	9	1	2
16.	$1\frac{1}{2}$	24	$1\frac{1}{2}$
17.	16	1	6
18.	3 x 3 x 3 x 3 x 3	12 x 12	6 x 6 x 6 x 6
19.	2^5	8^3	25^2
20.	16	343	27

	a	b
21.	E	(5, 3)
22.	A	(7, 5)
23.	D	(4, 8)
24.	C	(9, 1)
25.	B	(3, 6)

Final Test

Page 165

	a	b	c	d
1.	1220	2575	7936	94176
2.	13.512	8.331	494.492	4.32
3.	1000	700	3200	18000
4.	$1\frac{4}{15}$	$1\frac{7}{12}$	$1\frac{1}{2}$	$1\frac{1}{5}$
5.	24	21	8	36
	4	1	4	6

Page 166

6. 4.98   8.5   100   1.48
7. 494 cm   405 in.   59 m   10,800 ft.
8. P **9.** P
10. $\overline{PQ}$, $\overline{PR}$, or $\overline{PS}$
11. $\overline{RS}$ **12.** $\overline{RS}$ or $\overline{WX}$
13. 145° **14.** 35° **15.** 145° **16.** 35°
17. Y and W **18.** X, Z, M, N **19.** RST

Grade 6 Answers

Page 167

20. Rosetti
21. Tuesday
22. Thursday
23. 145
24.

Stem	Leaves
3	3 6 7
4	1 5 5 7 7 7
5	2 4

Key: 3 | 3 = 33

mean 44; median 45; mode 47; range 21

25. 9   4   7
26. 25   10   0
27. $1\frac{1}{2}$ 3 $\frac{1}{2}$
28. 8   3   14
29. *D*   **30.** *C*   **31.** *B*   **32.** *E*   **33.** *A*
34. (8, 7)   **35.** (4, 2)   **36.** (2, 7)   **37.** (5, 6)
38. (8, 3)

Page 168

39. 2,456; 94   **40.** $1\frac{1}{10}$ lbs.   **41.** $1\frac{5}{8}$ yds.

43. 22   **43.** 3,750 cu. m   **44.** $\frac{3}{8}$ $\frac{3}{16}$ $\frac{13}{16}$ **45.** 80%